FLIGHT FROM TH

BOOKS BY
LAURENCE LIEBERMAN

POETRY

Flight from the Mother Stone (2000)

The Regatta in the Skies: Selected Long Poems (1999)

Compass of the Dying (1998)

Dark Songs: Slave House and Synagogue (1996)

The St. Kitts Monkey Feuds (1995)

New and Selected Poems: 1962–92 (1993)

The Creole Mephistopheles (1989)

The Mural of Wakeful Sleep (1985)

Eros at the World Kite Pageant (1983)

God's Measurements (1980)

The Osprey Suicides (1973)

The Unblinding (1968)

CRITICISM

Beyond the Muse of Memory: Essays On Contemporary American Poets (1995)

Unassigned Frequencies: American Poetry in Review (1977)

The Achievement of James Dickey (1968)

Flight
from the
Mother Stone

POEMS BY

LAURENCE LIEBERMAN

The University of Arkansas Press
Fayetteville
2000

04   03   02   01   00   5   4   3   2   1

Designed by Liz Lester

⊛   The paper used in this publication meets the minimum requirements
of the American National Standard for Permanence of Paper for Printed
Library Materials Z39.48-1984.

Library of Congress Cataloging-in-Publication Data

Lieberman, Laurence.
        Flight from the mother stone : poems / by Laurence Lieberman.
                p.   cm.
        ISBN 1-55728-585-3 (pbk. : alk. paper)
        I. Title.
        PS3562.I43F58   2000
        811'.54—dc21   99-39102
                                                                CIP

"Eagle and Monkey" linocut by Laurence Donovan.

for Binnie,
    everlasting

ACKNOWLEDGMENTS

The author gratefully acknowledges the following journals in which these poems originally appeared:

The American Poetry Review: "Possum"
Arkansas Review: "Steps of the Snake"
Atlantic Monthly: "Love Nips of the Boa"
Boulevard: "A Gift for Granddad Jacob," "Of Fangs, Swipes from the Earth and Air"
The Caribbean Writer: "Four Sisters," "Moon Hole," "Ether"
The Chariton Review: "Boiling Lake," "Cactus Love," "Earth Kissed"
The Colorado Review: "To Merge With Trees," "Wild Donkey"
Crazy Horse: "Across the Starlit Dusk"
Denver Quarterly: "The Electrifier"
Five Points: "The She Babe," "The Warrior Priestess"
The Hudson Review: "The Diamond Miner and the Mermaid," "Wolf of the Skies"
Kenyon Review: "Flight from the Mother Stone," "Robbing the Queenies"
Michigan Quarterly Review: "Jawboners"
The New Republic: "Shore Derelict," "Hardhat Limbo"
The Ohio Review: "Grenada Birthday Song"
Pequod: "Pork Knockers, a Case of Sinusitis"
Prairie Schooner: "Purgatorio," "Fern Heaven"
River City: "The Divi-Divi Trees, Forsaken"
Sewanee Review: "Dueling U-Boats: Bonaire, 1944"
Shenandoah: "Jag," "Bonaire Sextet"
Southern California Anthology: "Sassy Belle"
Southern Review: "The Sacredness of Fingers"
Southwest Review: "The Lovesick Miner"
Tar River Poetry: "Epitaph for a Watering Hole"

"Voice to Voice" first appeared in the book *Influence and Mastery,* edited by Stephen Berg, Bedrock Books, Inc., Philadelphia.

The following poems were reprinted in *The World's Best Poetry*, edited by Harvey Roth: "A Gift for Granddad Jacob," "Cactus Love," "The Sacredness of Fingers," and "The Lovesick Miner."

Special thanks to the Center for Advanced Study and the Program for the Study of Cultural Values and Ethics at University of Illinois for creative writing fellowships which supported the completion of this book.

CONTENTS

I.

II.

III.

IV.

V.

I.

A GIFT FOR GRANDDAD JACOB

(Roseau, Dominica)

I.

Intertwined on the narrow second-story portico, Klaus
and Constable Mallory engage in a standup arm-wrestling
match . . . I'm diverted from my book and beer, seated

> at a table
> just inside the partition, their outdoors
> gallery a mere leg-length away:
> *Hey, watch it,* I yowl, fearful
> the taller man may flip the other
> over the flimsy guardrail to the traffic
> and pavement below. Gaunt angular Black Mallory,
> offduty policeman
> on Holiday, towers over Klaus—
> perhaps twice his age,
> the elder man buckling to his wobbly knees
> muttering soft curses under his breath
> in that thick German accent . . .
> But by a shrewdest whirlabout
> of footing, Klaus

throws the younger man off balance, his arms reversed
in a tangle, elbows aswerve. Dizzied and aghast, Mallory
flops to the floorboards on his hip, both men puffing

> for breath—
> cackles of hilarity, not anger, dump them
> loosely into one another's arms,
> a fraternal embrace . . . I'd started

to rise from my seat, perhaps to avert
a murder; but Christobel's hand on my shoulder
steadies me. *It's just their style of greeting,*
she says. *Some fun for them.*
Hah, see their smiles! Klaus always
wins. He fakes weakness,
then fools Mallory with trick moves. He's so fast,
I can't see how he does it. Klaus is full
of surprises, never the same
tactic twice, no repeats. Mallory,
who has a hefty

size-and-age advantage, shakes his brow. He's stumped.
Klaus is small-boned and wiry. *What gives here?* he chaffs.
Sure I had you that time . . . An avid student of Military

Science, Herr
Mallory loves to read War Sagas, and puts
himself under Klaus's tutelage.
So much more than a mentor!
He worships the agile Berlin expat
restauranteur, who had been for seven years
an officer and infantry trouble shooter in post-
war Germany's army . . .
Moments later, Herr Klaus, bowed
over the adjacent table,
begins drawing with a thick soft-leaded pencil
on a pad of legal-size memo papers.
Quick bold sketches of military
maneuvers are dashed off, vast legions
of men shifted

from side to side like pawns in a chess match. Mallory
asks a question or two, a sheaf of fresh sketches follow
by way of answer, sheets are ripped from the pad, crumpled

and strewn
about the floor. *You must stash* Mein Kampf
behind you, says Klaus, *and open*
your mind-set to THE SUBLIME.
Herr Rommel vas your true genius,
the military strategist par excellence. . . .
Now Klaus appears at my table, hand outstretched
in welcome (Do I hear
those heels click together?), while
glad Christobel mediates
between us, reciting my name, Klaus noted
owner of the Pub. Handshakes: half-risen
in my chair, half-seated still,
but Klaus's mood shift zips into gear,
silver-tinged eye

brows bunching up, thick close-cropped mustache aquiver,
and lips flying into a grimace (O my, I gave offense,
but how? Stung by my surname, I infer.) . . . *In auld Germany,*

ven I vas
a lad, I vas taught to rise from my chair
to greet my elders . . . But perhaps I
am your *Senior,* I coolly reply,
to which he guffaws. Our age numerals
bandied to and fro—he wins by a smidgin.
And I ascend, bidding him a second proper hello.
Vell, now I suppose
you'll be itching to lay the Hitler/
Third Reich guilt trip
on me. My Jewish friends are incorrigible
in fixing such blames. A heavy bore
it is . . . I wag my tousled head
Nay, for all demurral. Three shakes,
and we're gabbing

like old school chums. Soon I pick up vibes—our Christobel
and Klaus are doubtless a couple, her twenty years giving
his sixty-two a conjugal War of Nerves. She fell for him

the morning
they first met, she then sixteen & homeless,
jilted by her family, dapper Klaus
a new arrival from Europe.
Her petite features and kind eyes ideal
for hostessing, he hired her on the spot—
without references—to manage the bar and diner,
she to set up housekeeping
in the small one-room flat tucked behind
the floor-to-ceiling bar
mirror! Tough old bird, he was fast and rugged,
veteran of street-wars in Berlin city
strife . . . January had met
December. Whatever the age chasm,
it was a high-energy-

charge sweet match. He never came up short, whether in bed
or the run of domestic arts; but his constant mood swings
sent her reeling. Daily bouts of raging jealousy erupted,

tripped off
by any younger man she casually spoke to.
He begged her to marry him. *O hush,*
it's too soon to tie the knot,
she'd say, flattered, caressing his brow.
Later, maybe. Her whole life still ahead of her . . .
He'd gladly take her to Germany to meet his grownup
son and daughter, two grandkids—
and proud he'd be to show her off,
let any who may blink
at the clash of their ages and race mix. Here,

in Roseau, the locals abhor resident
               Whites, for all their sweet-talk
    at the diner. Still less, do they abide
      a mixed marriage.

No family to turn to on either side, this pair must face
a hostile daily flux of folks, but their love ever thrives
like an air-plant without roots. Self-fueled, they ignite.

    2.

Today, no more
      putting it off. Christobel
        must visit Granddad Jacob in prison, three months
    into his two year sentence
for smoking pot (just two small plants
      in the garden, barely enough to feed *his* habit:
        nobody else on Jacob's dope
          dole); to this day,
            neither family member nor friend
              has passed through
              the jail gates. High time it is for Granddad
        to get a little boost! Always before,
          she was turned back

by rigid guards,
      posted visiting hours nullified
        by her work schedule. At best, she'd leave a gift
    of fresh-picked fruit, candy,
or sweet cakes with the roguish Warden—
      who promptly filched them for his own private hoard.
        For all her efforts to assuage
          Grandsire's pain,
            no word of hers ever reached him,

her notes left
undelivered, never answered. Today, Sunday,
Klaus will put his *foot down*—click,
click of those heels—

upon my life
and honor, he'll boldly escort
his Christobel to jail; while I, too, a writer
must jump at this chance to see,
firsthand, *that loony bin of a lockup,*
a human barnyard and bullring: more animal
stockade than fitting quarters
for men—I must
see for myself to believe it.
O count me in,
I'm on board . . . Sergeant Mallory, no friend
to the current staff but a fellow
of their breed—cousin

in the soldierly
cloth—phones the prison ahead
to set a time for our visit: motley heterodox
party of four. Our request
flatly denied! Visiting hours, today,
are rescinded. A crisis in security. Worst
understaffing in many months:
too many guards
on sick leave, time off
for foreign
travel, a death in the family, or flat-out
malingering . . . It's a total shutdown
to the public,

and no exceptions
will be *brooked.* (Mallory's enraged,

that word *pisses* him off. *We're not even a river,*
stream, or deluge of guests,
just a damn brook, he groans—but hangs up
in defeat.) Now Klaus, a doer, never a quitter,
will have *none of this sass.*
He phones back,
turns on the same quixotic blend—
rancor & charm,
sledgehammer bluntness—that he worked off
on me when we first met, hours ago.
In six minutes,

we've settled on
an appointment time and strict code
number to meet a substitute foreman at the gate.
And we must be scrupulously
punctual, not one minute late *or* early
if we hope to gain admittance to the jail front
annex . . . Christobel fills
a small knapsack
with apples, bananas, mangoes,
& papayas. Off
we go! A chatty quartet. Mallory and I
installed in the rear bucket seats
of a four-wheel-drive

Pathfinder that's
equipped to plow through two-foot-deep
sinkholes of mud or quicksand, to ford shallow
river or dormant volcano
crater: all viable chances to be sure,
on this island. *Time is of the essence,* Klaus
chirps, as he hurtles us four
down the backalley
sidepath, shortcut to the uphill

wheelrut-gouged
zigzagging narrow two lane to prison . . . Slams
brakes in mid-turn. *Switch drivers! You
take the wheel, sweetie.*

3.

On a steep curvy ascent of road, Klaus swings
tall stick-shift to neutral, leaves motor idling, blinker lights
aflash: he tugs back the emergency brake (damn near
snaps it off!), and leaps out

the driver seat
beckoning to Christobel. *Now hurry up, please!
Today's the date, don't you know,
for the next driving lesson . . . But I hate
to drive,* she whimpers. *O take me
to visit my Gramps! . . .
Grab the wheel, or I turn back,*
he commands. *Now show
the men your stuff, girl!* Perhaps all
her driving lessons are threat-induced, our eyes agree,
Mallory and I.
We grip the door-frames, suck in

our breaths, and cheer her on. Her last hope
for reprieve, she squints back at Mallory—true Man of the Law—
and shouts: *I have no driver's license, nor learner's
permit . . . In that case, I assign*

*a Valid Permit
to you now,* he replies, shuffling in his coat
pocket for a notepad and pen.
TEMPORARY PERMIT to drive on this day,

May twenty, 1995, issued
to one Christobel.
Age twenty. Sight, twenty-twenty.
No misdemeanor.
No felony police record on file,
or hospitalized for mental breakdown in past five years.
You qualify.
So drive now, bids he, while Klaus,

snickering, concurs. She takes the outsize wheel
in both hands, unflicks the hand-brake with her knee, and kicks
the accelerator into a jump start. We buck, and lift
airborne for a prolonged moment—

small aircraft
on takeoff from a shrunk runway. She's floored
the foot pedal, and hip wriggles
first gear for extra heft; but Klaus's hand
grips the long vertical stick lever—
she hasn't learned
to do gearshifts yet, he admits.
And her two-fisted
grasp of the big wheel shows us!
No hands to spare for gear twists . . . *Brake/clutch, brake,*
now release both,
Klaus instructs, while he wields

the wobbly stick. Faster and faster she goes,
as steeper tilts the incline of roadway. No matter how sharp
the turn, she throws her shoulder into the wheel—
whipping it, always, in time

for Double-S
curves, while she swerves clear of the oncoming
traffic, her chin hitting the horn

with never a slowdown. Speed's now constant.
Road gradient, road angle, may vary
but pavement traveled
falls in with *her* commanding tempo—
never she with its
caprice. She—we must never forget—
is ROAD BOSS. *I can see we are in safe, O safest, hands*
says Mallory.
Three hands are better than two!

And I slowly peel my fingers from my eyes, peek
and peek again: we *are* safe, thanks to pilot and copilot equally
at the controls, her foot moves unerringly keyed to
Klaus's behest. *Clutch. Brake/*

clutch. But how,
I wonder, will she learn to drive by her lone
unaided wits, apart from this team
effort, twin moves: a duet, both pianists
at a single keyboard . . . She *steers*
by herself (God bless!),
I've never seen such acute bends
on two-way upgrade,
and we swoop to the jail doublegates
exactly on time, Klaus screeching, *Hit the damn brakes!*
one second before
we'd have rammed the howling guard.

4.

We four all pop out at once, four doors outswung, while the guard
untwists his face & learns
to breathe again—since our Christobel had all-but-pinned
him to the gates. He can't admit his fear, shock,

rage—for shame—so holds his tongue; he and Mallory exchange
        police badges,
    soon passing their respective palms to and fro
        across the metal plaques,
            checking, say,

for defect or counterfeit imprint, and it calms them both. Deputy
        Ralston now twirls his key
    in the flimsy shackle that secures those prison gates,
        one cheap cast-iron padlock: doors fly open
    and we step forward into a half-roofed anteroom, surprised
        to find ourselves
        the only visitors who have gained access
            on this Spring Sunday.
                Prison yard's

a wild melee of males, all suited in bluesy uniforms, some few
        twelve-year-old calves
    grazing the jail grounds beside eighty-year-old oxen.
        It's a human barnyard hodgepodge, no order
    or planned work detail in view: a minimum security lockup,
        all minor drug-
        busts or petty thieveries, I'd guess. Stabled
            in a narrow booth,
                we can see

most inmates through the upper stall, but they don't notice us,
        not expecting townsfolk
    today. Our escorts have abandoned us, Klaus jabbering
        all the while about *mean-spirited travesty:*
    the injustice of nailing seventy-five-year-old Granddad Jacob
        for that harmless
        habit he'd started fifty years back; in those days,
            it was legal and proper
                to smoke grass,

or grow it. *Vy don't they pick on blokes their own size,* he frets.
        Hah! They gave him a choice.
   Pay a twenty-thousand-dollar fine, or do two year's jail
      hard time: could be time off for good behavior,
  but nobody keeps close enough tabs on the men to say who gets
      an Early Pardon . . .
     At last, two guards route us to the GUEST ANNEX,
        half-enclosed, half-open
          at the top.

We straddle two benches, no seats with chair backs in this *parlor*
        hard-by the teeming jail
   courtyard, where the inmates ramble and circulate freely,
      no guards in range to monitor their safety—
  or ours, for all that. Christobel spots Granddad at the far end,
      who looks dizzy
     and confused. He's searching for something lost,
       or some*one*—you can discern
        he was briefed

that a family visit's in the offing, but his indifferent keepers
        have left him in the lurch.
   He's peering far and wide, but he moves in vague circles
      like a sheep or cow stung by electric prods,
  then turned loose to fare for itself in a wide fenced-in pasture.
      Christobel shouts
     his name and waves, but there's too much clamor,
       no outcries can reach him,
        and his sight's

too weak to see so far. *O what's become of his glasses,* she wails,
        and bursts into tears. Klaus,
   fuming, bickers with the office functionary in charge,
      who argues: *You must complete all paperwork*
     first, before any meetings with convicts may transpire. Today's

no blithe prison
holiday. . . . Constable Mallory's no help, he's back
    at the gateway, clowning
      with his newfound

police crony; I'm left to pat Christobel's back and mumble words
    of false comfort, a half-hour
    lost to these paltry meanderings. By chance, the old man
      rambles within earshot, we all roar his name,
    he seems to hear and swerves in our direction; a hopeful glimmer—
      if fleeting—plays
    about his eyes, but a concrete pillar obtrudes
      between him & his honey,
        blocks the view . . .

I switch bench spaces with Christobel, but that imposing column
    keeps jumping in the way
    for all my maneuvers, as if an unseen puppeteer jiggles
      the two searchers to *just miss* making eye
    contact, while Granddad keeps following the line of commotion.
      At last, a guard
    squires him to the obscure entryway; he stumbles,
      and trips sideways into her;
        they're hugging

and sighing before he sees her face—chants of each other's names
    ripple through the dank air . . .
    Three prison staff spring forward. Where were they hidden
      before? Now they take a high profile interest,
    all three sneering at Christobel as if she's Granddad's hussy,
      a common slut,
    not his family at all. Two more guards commence
      to search Klaus & me—
        O suddenly

it dawns on them we might be smuggling illegal drugs or weapons,
      a total frisking, O Lord!
   they stop just short of a strip-search. We're viewed
    as mere jail chaff ourselves, and I can feel
my citizen status falling away like yesterday's deodorant.
     The office chief—
   who'd quarreled with Klaus before—now proclaims
    a five-minute time allotment
      for our visit

shall be enforced, all that remains of the prescribed sad half-hour.
    We should've begun our chat
sooner, instead of *frittering away* our time. Poor Klaus
   is beside himself with pleas and near-threats . . .
Christobel passes a sack of fruit to Granddad, who crookedly grins
    at big fresh apples,
   revealing only two upper teeth intact—no way
    can he munch those red beauties,
      kin of her heart.

WORK CHANTS
OF THE DIAMOND MINER

I. Of Fangs, Swipes from the Earth and Air

Their first time out, all fledgling
gold-and-diamond miners are provided with cost-free passage
on amphibious transport planes to Guyana's
harsh interior. Seatless,
those aircraft rattle and buck in the least headwind,

the maximum capacity fourteen men squeezed
shoulder to shoulder—
seven on each side—hunched down
low on that furrowed
aluminum floor,
no baggage racks above
or room in the hold for personal gear.
Many sit on small dufflebags . . .
On his first day, Chico,
age twenty,
arrives at dusk. He sleeps three hours
in the hammock strung out
between two jungle pines—a small lantern

suspended overhead. When the gong
is struck at midnight, or earlier, he hears a frantic scraping
of men lighting damp matches on their helmets
or belt buckles. A few wicks
flare out: torch by torch lights up, for none dares lower

a foot in the dark, in fear of swift death
that slithers, crawls

or drags its menacing half-
raised tail in the air
below. To sleep
near earth—whether on a cot
or pallet—is death. Quick tarantulas
and scorpions abound thereon,
whose bite or sting razes
a man's limb,
speedy amputation often *a must* . . .
But Labaria, the WHITE
CURSE, is terror to miners. All-but-certain

demise, Pit Viper Labaria's *wet*
puncture (rare *dry* bites, if the snake's venom gland was drained
recently, or if he oddly chooses to deliver
a benign peck—dry *love nip*—
as often his wont, survival is a good chance): the victim

foams white sudsy discharge from eyes, ears,
& nose, his tongue swells
to three times its normal size—
followed by choking fits
or worse, spinal
seizures, whichever comes first.
In some cases, whitish drool might leak
from all of the body's pores
cocooning the flesh
in a gauzy
insulation of snow-white slime . . .
Rabies and Lockjaw
all rolled into one albino second-skin rind.

Vipers, scorps, and the eight-legged
furballs besiege the diamond miner's river-bank terrain, much
as roaches infest a rancid grease-caked kitchen.

Ground zero, by dark, is barefoot
doom; unbooted footfall, true suicide . . . All such warnings

                  pale beside the fate of Chico's first-week
                      tent mate who, ignoring
                  all safety imperatives posted
                  on every Nth tree trunk
                    like FBI ten-
                most-wanted mug shots,
        drops bare foreleg from his hammock
        before striking a match & takes
            savage nick on his tough
                  foot heel skin
      callus . . . the Viper's tooth needling
                into that thick crust,
which slows down the advance of the poison,

    but to no avail. He clings to life
for five ghastly hours: the swelling, fevers, and convulsions
     until—at last—that telltale white exudate
       comes oozing from every orifice.
There's no antidote for that single lethal skin prick.

          Viper strikes in the face or neck are best;
                dying comes quick, less
            than a minute's delay at most.
             But those darting hits
                  to extremities—
             even fingertip or toe—
      are always fatal, the prolonged deaths
        most agonizing. Amputation's
            ever too late to stanch
               the killer flow;
      once venom enters the bloodstream,

there's no stopping it . . .
In response to Mervyn's gruesome slow dying,

Chico hankers to quit the mines
for months—but stays. He'll make his own truce with Pit Vipers,
never tempting them with a patch of bare skin
dangled within tooth-pierce range . . .
For seven years, he sticks out the miner's hack-and-chop

derby—it becomes second nature to step clear
of any ground nippers;
but he falls prey, at long last,
to the lighter-than-air
hypodermic
beaked vermin, hang-glider
assassins of the wind. One such strafer
mosquito, squirming between pleats
of full-surround overhead
netting, pounces
on his pillowed cheek in sleep. Fevers
and chills—grave malaria
takes its toll. Longtime survivor of the worst

known Labaria and scorpion hordes
in the Americas, he is taken out by a diaphanous-winged speck
of flying tissue . . . Though in remission, Chico's
always at risk—malarial for life,
one bout of flu or grippe can revive the sleeping microbe.

2.   *The Lovesick Miner*

From his twentieth
birth season, plucky Chico labored in the river mines
of Guyana's dark
interior, working both on shore bank pits

and in deep tunnels coursing below
the river floor. A certified diver, he would often plunge
seventy feet
to reach the gash excavated by jawlike toothy cutters
dragged, in turn, by those wide

boxy barge-ships.
Fifty-year-old all-wood dredge boats, they were built
to last hundreds
of years from *greenheart* woods—the toughest
grain whose resins grow ever more strong
with aging, impervious to any corrosive agents, whether
timber-eating
mineral acids contained in the natural river brines
or worst chemicals employed

in gouging out
mine shafts: wood grown more acid-resistant than steel . . .
By his own choice,
the youth worked night shifts for double pay;
and whether he plied his hatchets, power
drills, and pickaxes underground or underwater, his face-
mask torchlight
was the sole beacon that illuminated his passage:
it afforded enough semblance

of day to keep
him alert & hacking his thirty rock feet of burrow-dig-
per-night session.
If the kerosene oil burner in his helmet
snuffed out (fuel leak or dislodged
wick), his FAILSAFE—waterproof battery-driven generator—
would kick in
for long enough to bolster his escape from peril
of losing his way in earthen

or watery cul-
de-sacs, by tumbling ashore or aground. But the weeks
of all-nighters,
no vacations or sickleave, were palliated
by his happy previsions of daybreak.
Such joy it was to glide to river surface from the depths
at shift end
and greet the knife-edge horizon of first light.
He'd relish his upcoming romp

over riverside
bluffs, to gather those shimmery yellow wildflowers
(daisies, he called
them, but pretty weed blooms would be more
on the mark): the merest glimmerings
of half-light grazed the hill crests as fond Chico gamboled
like goat or fawn
over the grassy slopes, and garnered each morning's
bouquet to mail to his sweetheart,

Amolly, in far-off
Georgetown. Then he stole back to his low-pitched tent
to script flowery
brush strokes of thick calligraphic letters
to his *flame-for-life*, flower blossoms
pressed close in many-layered packets (onionskin, to keep
the air-weight down);
he composed songs and verses with each missive, hand
carried to the little seaplane

Postal Airboat
that ferried his mail, the tiny airstrip just one mile
from the diamond
mines, and delivery port next door to Amolly's
urban cottage. One day's hiatus, no more.

What luck! She wrote back, if only half so often, keeping him
primed for the brutal
hours of his lightless dark shifts—he never guessing
the chill-out of her wastrel heart.

3.   *Pork Knockers, a Case of Sinusitis*
     (Bartica Diamond Mines, Guyana)

    Pork knockers. Six races, drawn
from all classes of Guyana's coast towns, came
    to work in the Bartica Mines:
Asians, Hindus,
        Africans, Whites, and Amerindians
            found a common bond in the one food staple,
        cheap & tough-rinded, ever-durable, misshapen flat hunks
            of salted pork. Like our beef jerky
or *chawing* tobacco, today, both food
and stimulant—the tangy flavor and aroma gave the men
a low high charge that lasted out
    their sixteen hour work shifts in the gold mines,
        or diamond mines. The Black Man was the classic Pork Knocker—
hence museum statuettes in dark face, honoring
that special breed of man.

                    African stock
            seemed best inured to the tough,
                    gross work detail
            of the miner's relentless brute hours . . .
                    Drill-and-hack, chop-
            and-grind, till a man feels it's his own dry-
                            bones skeleton
                he scrapes and mauls for the last
                marrow-deep snippets of ore. Gold ore.
    Diamond nuggets . . . How do you know one from the other?

I ask my companion. *You don't.*
They can be layered, one upon the other, mixed
in a single shovel's unearthing
of cracked stone
        shards . . . The other races do seem
                to succumb to mine ills—flus, animal stings—
            far quicker than the Blacks. Chico, our East Indian lad,
                was no exception. So frequently he was
    laid up with croups, bronchial colds, and worst-
    case sinusitis: his head felt like a thick bee-hive stuffed
with mounds of rancid honey.
    For weeks at a time, he forgot he had nostrils
    or nasal passages, so plugged were his skull vents—his mouth
often agape, sucking for least breath. But his grueling
dig hours never let up.

                        No sick leave
                allowed, his meager salary
                        would be docked
            double for hours missed. Sleep frazzled
                        by blocked sinuses
        for five straight days, Chico wandered off
                        one afternoon—
            between two night shifts. Knapsack
            over his shoulder, canteen tied to belt,
    he would seek out the Piai Man, sage elder Occultist

    of the near forest tribe, encamped
some ten miles back in the Interior. Most Hindus
    and tribespeople, though at odds
in lifestyles,
        often converge in trials of the Spirit.
        This Piai man, a shrunken wizard in his Nineties,
        hobbled on two canes—but wielded them with strong overhand
            chops, like a skier trekking on ski poles.

He led poor snuffling Chico to a cavern
in the rock wall, and bade him to lie supine on a hammock
propped on two Y-shaped fence posts
beside a wide-lipped cauldron. Thereupon, he mixed
a rich concoction of roots, tubers, herbs & powders in the dark
briny waters of the pot, soon lighting a tall fire
under the great clay boiler

shakily mounted
on four cast-iron legs. In moments,
the glowing kettle
was bubbly and discharging a rich mist
of aromatic fumes,
whereat the Piai instructed Chico to inhale
long slow draughts
of the reddish steam and hold
each sucked-in breath for a full minute,
or until sneezing fits overcame him. Within an hour,

Chico's sinuses cleared, his nasal
breathing returned to normal for the first time
in many months . . . Then Piai crossed
the youth's palm
with a brown seed-pod amulet, oval shaped,
the size of a large walnut. The pod would bring
good luck, he said, but should be kept on Chico's person
at all times, even during sleep—whether
it be stuffed in pajama pocket, or taped
to his abdomen. The pod was oddly lightweight, but so tough
was its outer shell, a common nail
would snap in two pieces before a hammer's blows
could drive it through the pod's rind. All such pods had fallen
from flowering trees in Trinidad and Haiti—no other
islands their source. Each fall,

                              they were swept
                  out to sea, some few washing ashore
                              with the high tides
                  of the full moon rolling into Guyana's
                              Southern strand. Piai's
            disciples made pilgrimage to gather the faded
                              brown egg shapes
                  each autumn—October the month
                  of most frequent pod finds. A good beach
harvest might turn up dozens of those migrant pebbly

        hollows—at best a cluster stacked
    in piles like so many *gouged Asian eyeballs*, wind-
        rolled into heaps. More usually,
    they were scarce
            and hard to come by. Those apprentice Piais
                might scour the shoreline for days, before stumbling
                upon even one good-luck bubble pod. *Here, keep this nearby.*
                I see bleak waterways ahead for you, warns
    Piai . . . No believer in charms or magic
    keepsakes, Chico nearly spurned the gift but caught himself—
he bowed, warmly smiling his thanks,
        not wishing to seem rude to his proven healer.
        Then, absently, he'd tuck the pod in his pants-cuff or rolled-up
shirt sleeve: rarely in the same place twice, he kept it
near at hand always, never lost,

                              never misplaced,
                  amazingly, for many months . . .
                              When your luck's
                  down or spirit is low, saith his Piai,
                              rub the pod quickly
                  between your two palms. It'll heat up promptly
                              and hold warmth
                  like a Thermos, also cleaving

to the good luck charge for many hours . . .
Humbled by that fierce heat power, he grew to respect

the amulet—no true devotion
or faith, but a guarded trust. In some crises,
it could help. Chico mustn't
write it off . . .
A year later, freed of any sinus attacks
and praiseful, often, for the Piai's art of healing,
the miner and four river-bottom-dig cronies found themselves
one stormy day to be puffily oar-paddling
a speedboat—whose motor had sputtered
to a halt—into a turbulent rapids on the Mazaruni River.
The gale-churned currents ran wild
and spun their long-nosed craft in wicked circles.
The vessel's bow got snared in a grooved slot of sub-surface rock
and cracked the sleek frame down to the keel, whipping
the five paddlers helplessly

overboard, two
still queerly swiping away
with their blade-
shafts of pinewood at the Seven Winds
as they flew sideways
into the river maelstrom. Chico lost sight
of his comrades,
all sucked under moiling surf-spray,
he alone crab-clawing momentary toehold
on a mossy sloped rock: bastion shortlived, he flipped

off into a whirl of wave crests
and gave himself up for doomed! Swallowing big gulps
of water, he sang mantras & chants
to the beckoning
afterlife, when the magic seed-pod leapt

into his hand from uncurling shirt sleeve; suddenly,
he was targeted by Piai's blazing eyes, whose balloon of face
hovered just inches over the water before him
signaling with its jaw twist to the left
a jutting verge of shoreline. Chico had given himself over
to the ghost couriers of Death,
but those riveting eyes of the Piai steered him
back to a safe haven of shore-weed fronds, sparking a new bout
of swim-strokes in him. Swerving toward shore, he clung
to long tufts and spears of beach

grasses, yanking
himself to safety on a reef-
edge, soon after
grappling his gold-and-diamond dig mates,
one by one, from below.
Each face, in turn, bespoke it had met Death
and acquiesced,
but tumbled back into life's brief
interlude—no clue to the fateful reprieve . . .
Wave-top flicked the lucky pod from Chico's lax grip.

4. *The Diamond Miner and the Mermaid*
    (Mazaruni River, Guyana)

Crossovers.
Hindus and Amerindians both worship that woman
of the sea: the Mermaid, patron saint
and wrathful angel, by turns.
To the native rainforest tribes, she's
Water Mama. She has pervasive—if limited—
powers. Gales and hurricanes, all storms spawned
at sea, are her bailiwick.
Her Theater in the Round. No fewer
than nine known sects

pay her tribute, offerings wafted into the winds
or sprayed upon the rivers—on holidays.
                    To the Hindus, as well, she's
Mother Ganga. All powerful. River
        omnipotent. She,

and she only, rules these feisty waters.
    On sacred days,
            aged crones, young lovers, chambermaids,
                small children of Hindu caste—
            all hasten to the seawall near Georgetown at daybreak,
    or *before* first light, to bestrew fresh-picked

                        wildflowers
            and fruits upon the river's currents. They moan
                chants, or recite brief ancient verses,
        as they scatter their ritual
                    gifts to Mother Ganga. She, of the acrid-
    smelling broad-finned scaly fish tail, presides
                over the lives of Guyana folk, and often invades
            their dreams . . . The morning
after his long night's dig & dredge
                of the river bottom
            diamond mines, young Chico dropped in the mirror-
    calm Mazaruni a hook baited with black-haired
                    many-legged tarantulas (scooped
        from his tent floor with a tin cup),
        and then commenced

his three-hour siesta. He'd forgotten
    the cork-bobbered
            line, when he awoke to a gurgly churning
                of currents beside his river's-
            edge tent stakeout. He absently raised knotted twine
from the shore bank, and drew against a fierce

tugging . . . yanked up
by the rosy-jagged gills a record-size Lou-Lou.
This thirty-pound giant catfish spun
about in wild flapping gyrations,
touching its tail to rubbery long snout,
repeatedly, during those convulsive heaves
to escape. The agile youth slowly lifted his catch
from the bankside gulf,
amazed at the Lou-Lou's thick girth—
he stood poised to twist
the hook from its bony jaws with his pocket pliers
when the portly fish shot upward like a rocket
discharged from its booster. He swung
awry, finding that tent mate Curzon,
stout Venezuelan

immigrant, had snared his prize catfish
with savage meat-hook
through its belly, knowing pal Chico meant
to throw the colossal fish back
into the briny river-scum surface unwounded, as he'd
always done before. Vegetarian and kind-hearted

soul that he was,
the Hindu miner would never trap—much less kill—
wild beings that flourished in wind,
earth, or waters: bird, rabbit, fish . . .
Yet his peer, Curzon, had swept the Lou-Lou
away before Chico could gasp, or blare out
his protest. No matter, it's a mere fish, he consoled
himself; but that evening,
the scariest dream of his life
befell him. Mother Ganga,
bare-breasted and crowned with a diamond tiara, came

to him: afloat in the tent space over his head,
          she held up two mammoth Lou-Lous
     on short fish stringers, and bespoke
          sad omens. He, Chico,

the one loyal guardian of God's creatures
     in the miner's camp,
          would be held *to blame, to blame. Take heed!* . . .
          He'd worked in the diamond mine
     which had disgorged some of the bulkiest uncut gemstones
in the world over the past five years—the mermaid's

               jewels seemed drawn
          from that stock. The largest gems in her necklace
               were still jagged-edged, raw diamonds
     in the rough; they had the translucent
               glaze of beauty unrefined, and some flashed
with a haunting neonesque half-light. But stones
               in her coronet were cut and honed to a perfect scale
          of finish. And so taken
was he with the pulsing of those
               many-faceted brilliants
          encircling her brow and hung from her neck, he hardly
     noted, at first, that her long ruffled white dress
               fell across a great broad fish tail
          that burgeoned from her hips. It curled
          upwards at the bottom,

and waggled back and forth as she spoke.
     She hovered in air
          above his hammock, the two immense fish dangled
               over his brow. She scolded him
          for laying a fish trap, hairy-legged spider bait tossed
casually into the river for *cruel sport*. Chico,

of all people!
He alone—among the miners—evinced a spirit
of caretaking toward most animals
which abounded near the camp base.
His fellow diamond miners, one and all,
rapaciously scavenged the forest creatures
and fish; thus, she gave Chico notice that the time
for the group's comeuppance
was at hand. So he should take heed—
be forewarned of just deserts
she would soon dole out. Then she wept beady tears,
in grief for the dead & wounded beasts—they fell
to her breast, drop by drop, like lumps
of molten ore and sizzled, steamily,
on her pale skin

as she crooned her warnings . . . He awoke,
shuddering. Her figure
had vanished, but the two fish hung suspended
where she left them, slick scales
gleaming for some minutes before his wide-awake trance.
He blinked, fiercely, until they too faded from view,

sighing with relief
as one who had stared down a sick hallucination.
But he spent hours fearfully alert,
wary lest those accusing fish shapes
reappear, whether in sleep or waking dream.
Then forgot . . . Two weeks slipped past. And without
a moment's warning, brutal wind-storm struck the river.
Choppiest waves, ever,
swept the surface, and currents
ran amok, fierce whirlpools
winding around the miners' two bargelike dredge boats.
The eddies kept reversing spin direction, heaving

the boats this way and that, each vessel
tilting more and more, skippers battling
at the controls—

but keels upended and sank, three divers
drowning in last ditch
plummets to save the ships . . . Days before,
Chico had warned the mine bosses
about his dream omens, but they scoffed at his *sissyish*
ravings—and fell victim to the Dark Angel's curse.

II.

SHORE DERELICT

They call him Watras (Capybara his textbook
name)—perhaps a shortened form
of water rat, since he's
always prowling
along the river banks or creek margins. Watras,
the bulkiest
rodent in the world and, for his size,
much the slowest.
A clumsy gait, he has. Mostly
a grass eater

himself, not much chance to be a carnivore
if all smaller game can outrun
and outwit you. Even so,
his ratlike snout
and furtive shambling trot roused fear or malice
in the hearts
of transient fisherfolk who settled
in riverside camps.
Thus, for a few generations
five-shilling

bounty was levied on their heads, and scads
of hunters massacred Watras
for coins. So plentiful
were the rodents,
you could amass a reeking stockpile of carcasses
in one morning's
quick sweep of the littoral environs,
and carry back home
your day's fair wage . . . But today,
this long-haired

wide-nosed rat, slinky Watras, has caught on
as great succulent food-fad
with the local riverside
homesteaders, who
scorch & roast them like wild boars on twisting
spits upraised
over open-hearth smoky pine fires,
their flesh flaking
sweetly like salmon . . . *Endangered*
species—Watras.

LOVE NIPS OF THE BOA

Secret despoiler of herds,
he works by guile and cunning. Noiseless,
with hardly a flicker of overt motion in attack,
he starves the calves by siphoning off—in shrewd calm,
that numbing soothe and hypnotic caress—the milk of mothers . . .
The slithering boa glides through knotholes in pineboards, barely
rustles the dense haystack it pierces, and comes up under
the half-asleep cows to stroke their bloated udders
with gentlest forked-tongue lappings; bovine
light sleepers that might be blasted
from a lull of slumber's

trance by least skirry
of field mice brushing their forelegs
or tails, now drawn from sleep into uttermost
removes by this gentlest slurp & suction, baby calf's
touch never so rhythmic and lightly stupefying. Mother cows
cannot know how it is that they're swiftly milked, O resistlessly
depleted and robbed of their throbbing loads. Amazing it be,
so small of mass are the boas, but they can engorge
their swelled tubular length to nearly double-
thick expanse of their normal girth
with the imbibed milk,

as if they've swallowed
a whole litter of baby rabbits, coons,
or possums in a few gulps—as well they might.
A boa's whole body is a throat. Its brain is so far
uptunnel from its tail, one end ignores the other's limits—
stuff, stuff it in: that's the only message! Then, lumbering away
like a gluttonous skunk or possum that has supped on twice

its body weight, the boa drags its overstuffed yards-
long belly, then burrows under the haystack
to hiddenly sleep off its gorged daze
of satiety . . . The farmers,

distraught by those false
milkings, freakish drainoff of prize
cows' mammaries, guess the culprits. They sweep
sharp-edged machetes through suspicious long bulges
under barnstraw, a wavering or trembling of the haypiles
as if the hay itself took breath: insucks & outflows, faint wave
motions rippling across low flat haystack is the giveaway . . .
Cutlass slashes dozing snake's milk-pouchy innards,
clipped sides twitchy like two live offspring—
but no, they're dying severed pipe lengths
stunned into a death dance.

JAG

            We slouch past the jaguars
        and boa constrictors, penned
        in oddly juxtaposed cages—both touted
as menacing foes
    to Guyana cowherds.
       They're lucky to be behind bars—
       for on the loose,
they'd soon fall prey to the cattle farmer's
bullet or machete . . . When jaguars lay siege to a ranch,
        they single out
         all young or sickly calves for attack:
    most powerful cats

            in the world, their jaws
        strong enough to crush the skulls
        of baboons or bears five times their weight
and bulk. Lying still
    as stone for hours, crouched
        on tree limb or low cliff ledge,
      they spring upon
backs of the grazing herd—they can plunge
forty or fifty meters and always land on their prey
        with precise aim
        of diving hawks, then gnash the skulls
    or spines of victims

            in seconds. To intercept
        marauding jaguar, the huntsman
        would have to nail it airborn with rifle shot
or arrow—there's no way
    to save a calf once the jag
        has struck, touching claw or tooth

to loping back.
Like the fox who raids a chicken-coop, jaguar
strikes with bold forthright pounce. Ranchers gun him down,
       set bait in traps,
          freeze up his arteries with rat poison,
   or catch him in snares. . . .

VOICE TO VOICE

The macaw does his full lineup of tricks
to please Chico. These two magic-
makers, man and bird,
have teamed up
before. You can read the glimmers of rapport
in their eye-
flash simpatico. When young Chico
hums a brief tune,
his feathered mimic chatters
back; tongue clicks

rouse like-sounding throaty squawks. Tuning
up, they could be an ensemble
of two instruments, as
far removed
as cello and bassoon, say, but the crazily mis-
matched voices
flirt with each other, toying
with near octaves.
Then, after many little shifts
of fine cueing,

they groove in sync. Chico signals by finger
wave, and the wide-faced parrot
(its owlish skull broader
than its wing-
folded torso) hops on jointed-twig toes across
the cyclone
fence cage mesh, twirls, and hangs
upside down. Next,
he wags that inverted oval
of wry face back

and forth, abrupt swings like the pendulum
  of a Grandfather Clock. *Now dance,*
O dance, says glad Chico,
  and Macaw
obeys, bobbing up and down, while revolving big
lowered beak
  in narrow circles—he keeps time
    with his mentor's
finger snaps, blithe shut-winged
live metronome

                dangled in place. His yellow stripes flare out,
                    clashing wildly with his feathers'
                            royal blue sheen, flamy
                                yellow bands
                circling his eyes. He shrieks joy from cage roost,
                                he and Chico
                    intertwined in voice-to-voice relay
                                act. It's a shared
                    zingy high—man to bird margins
                                wane and vanish. . . .

ROBBING THE QUEENIES

I.

Two senior
Grenada ladies and I, singly,
spring from adjacent circular stairwells
at once: three sea moles rising from our hull burrows
just moments after nightfall.
A sublimely pellucid star-burst sky! But that's not what stuns
us, and holds us unspeakably
in trance, we three alone on the Carriacou
Ferry's poop deck.
Great streaks of light surge and glimmer, wheeling
over the creamy

sea surface
glaze—many long arcs running
parallel, as if flaming in formation,
while others blaze a solo course. I'm struggling to name
this fine brilliance, sky flash.
Near kin to lightning, but it's too localized over surface luster,
hovery. No thunder. No storm
threat. *Lowest heat lightning I ever saw,* I say.
Both old gals break up
in titters. *No way! It could be the work of sorcery,*
whether shaman

or mad sinner.
You never know if the spirits be
helpers or demons, when they play light tricks
before our eyes, perhaps to lure us to hopelessly downslide

into the Black Pit! . . . My eyes

betray my fear. I'm easy prey to myths or tales of *a haunting*.

More giggles, laughing out. *O see*

them come now! says the tall smarter lass.

What a spectacle it is.

Six or seven fleet lights whirling over the swells

in perfect sync

like color bands

of a rainbow—at such close range,

they do seem to radiate a flux of shifting

colors. *They are luminous,* she says. A rare—if punctual—

school of high-flying fish

that choose only one time of year to do their leaps from this bay.

They are reputed to adroitly dance

and twirl in place on their tails, but today,

as we plainly see,

they hurtle against the tides to reach the other side

of the channel.

2.

"This night is special to us. When the flying fish

leap forth in great numbers,

as now, it's a tipoff—a signal

we watch for

every year. Always it comes

between mid-September

and October-end. Our great old *Sea*

Mamas (still fertile breeders, some well past

their hundredth year) shall waddle

ashore on Carriacou's remotest strand

to build their nests and lay hundreds of eggs in one day—

if unbothered by hunters . . .

We poachers hide in the cave mouth near shore,
                    watch them crawl

over the narrow blacksand beach to leaf cover:
          they pause and look about,
                    seem to reflect upon possible
                              interlopers,
                    then pick a site and begin
          to root around—they dig
          with their back legs and tails. We keep
a hush, and wait them out. Stay alert we must,
          day and night, or some others
                              may come and snatch our finds: we, the first
                    here, must guard our just reward, so we spell each other.
                    When Eunice sleeps, I double
                    my keen eyeful, she the same if I doze off. Our
                    snoozes be brief,

not to overtax the partner. Best to let post-
          partum turtle moms take
                    their sweet ease and lounge, groggily,
                              in a swoon
                    of exhaustion. O wait for them
          to wobble hither and yon,
          for a week perhaps, and meander back
to sea. But if other egg poachers come puttering
          within range, we make a dash
                    and break for the nests. When we snatch
                    the eggs, the Queenies start beating the sand, wildly,
                    with winglike flippers, and swish
                    thick waves of sand-spray across the distance
                    into our faces,

blindingly. Their aim is amazing, catching us
          in the eyes whichever

way we turn, to escape their flings.
　　　It's futile
　　　to flinch—if they're within range,
　　we're trapped, who crave prize
　　eggs. We have no choice but to sneak up
on the seesawing four-legged shell, so to catch it
　　unawares as it basks
　　　　　in tidal pools. We two must grasp it up
　　　　from both sides at once, and quickflip the creature over
　　　　on its back, disabling
　　　　those madly flapping leg-webs, while staying clear
　　　　　of the beak's

nasty swipes and tail's whiplash. *O heave,* I say.
　　Heave-ho! And we muster
　　　our strength for back-wrenching hoists
　　　　to wangle
　　　　the flapjack deadweight of shell
　　to come about on its back.
　　Not blinded yet, we pause to flush the sand
from our eyes, and get on with the egg-heist, filling
　　our net bags with more sheer poundage
　　　　of thin-shelled eggs than we can safely drag,
　　　　much less carry, without bursting much of the sweet brood.
　　　　Three or four trips, it may take us,
　　　　to wholly scoop out and excavate the deep-gouged
　　　　　pit she has dug."

　3.

　　　　I cry *"Foul!*
　　　Heartless and unfair it is, to leave
　　those poor huge briny sea-fossils out to rot
on their backs—their bellies, at last, to be pecked apart

by diving hawks." "No problem,"
they reply. "We take care to pitch her back upright after that egg
haul, and then we guide her—step
by trudging slow step—back to the shorelines." So
confused is her sense
of direction, dizzied from hours on her back, she needs
re-routing. Then,

too, they feel
they must nudge her to scurry back
to sea. Failing that, the next day's earliest
beachcombers, or the homebound fisher fleet, finding turtle
stranded helpless on her back,
will nab her for her soup meat. Yes, take the life of this Duchess,
brazen old survivor sow,
just for a few tender ounces of belly flesh
to flavor our soup!
Ranking dowager of the Antilles, she must deserve
a kinder fate.

How demeaning
for her lovely grizzled neck leather
and barnacle-laden, grit-and-brine-tattooed
patchwork of shell to be hastily stripped and dumped, O left
to knock about on shore rocks
for months, swept aimlessly by the tides like mangled flotsam
or driftwood. Far better to send
her back to those deepsea haunts, her fond refuge,
and she'll return
to deposit fine bumper egg-crops for thirty seasons
more, without lapse . . .

Grand Lady, she,
Jolene and Eunice cherish her eggs
above all others—chicken, duck, goose: none

can compare. Her fecund brood surpasses even much-touted
quail eggs, or pheasant eggs,
for softness and sweet flavor when poached. *The children go crazy*
for them. Ah, best they be
for young bones stretching out long so quick
you blink twice
at daybreak—your kid grew inches overnight. And best,
too, for long life.

WOLF OF THE SKIES

Half-avian,
half-human: vampiric
birds of prey who inhabit
a nethermost circle of Dante's
INFERNO—those shrewish female killer birds—
witness the Harpies! . . . Giant
high-fliers
of the dark forested
Americas, the largest eagles
in the world—
Harpies nest only in the tallest of trees,
trees with the widest upper limb
spreads: Silk-Cottonwoods
whose topmost

branches provide space for that five-foot-
diameter nest
expanse, which accommodates Harpy babes'
huge wing spans. Mama Harpies
go after small mammals, mostly: wild spider monkeys,
snakes & iguanas their favorite prey, to feed

the fledgling
chicks. Nesting on one egg
at a time, a single-child brood—
they're a rarity, even among eagles
and the nobler hawks . . . The hunting mother
hides, amazingly, in thick patches
of fern-tree fronds,
or behind wide-leafed vines
that wrap around the trunks. Hardest
to conceal

are those elongated turbanlike heads, necks
encircled by wide ruff of purply-
gray feathers that ripple
in wind chops,

puffed out in curly spirals . . . She's dubbed
the Flying Wolf
by Amerindian tribes of Guyana's interior,
who dread her rapacious
pounce. Cruising at high altitudes that test the limits
of human sight, she swoops, diving so fast we glimpse

a wing-folded
slender pointy-beaked blur.
A Harpy's been spotted picking off
two small monkeys at once, transversely
streaking across the upper branches of a tree
in a single parabolic arc:
one nestled
in her beak, the other
braced in talon's clutch—her aim
so precise
she hardly flicked a leaf or branch en route . . .
Often, she'll carry squealing charge
some twenty miles back
to her eyrie,

for quick deposit in gaping maw of her long-
pinioned gawky
newborn. And oddly harrowing it is to hear
distant shrieks of a captured
monkey, rabbit, possum, or squirrel grow swiftly near
before you track the soaring Harpy's approach

as she cruises
overhead, nestward bent.
The panic in those cries raises
a listener's hackles like the siren
of a far-off ambulance, too suddenly looming
close to home—followed by relief
of its darting
past, when it fades to shrill
whistle trailing off in the opposite
direction . . .
Whenever the natural wild game grows scarce
for nesting Harpies of the South
Kanuku Mountains, famished
eagles may drop

out of the skies without warning and snatch
human toddlers
from a family campsite at midday, ignoring
the howls, stomps, and arm-wavings
of nearby parents. The abducted child, never saved
nor any but his scoured-clean bones recovered,

prompts instant
posse of best archers
to embark on eagle-search junkets.
That crew of huntsmen, by Tribal Oath,
are sworn to bring down the Wolf of the Skies
before they return home, hitting near-
impassable trails
for weeks or months. If need be,
they scout for telltale nests in highest
Silk-Cottonwoods.
Once the crownlike thick eyrie is ferreted out,
they hurriedly piece together vine-

                                            woven sheets of foliage
                                                for concealment,

dig burrows, and lay themselves out flat
        under the cloaks—
                stakeout's never too near the nesting tree
                    or a restless, squawky nursling
                might tip off the homebound mother that their ambush
        lurks close. Patience & soft breathing. Late or soon,

                                                swift huntress
                                        carrying the fresh-caught
                                    wriggly burden will glide down
                                to feed her hungry eaglet. Alighting
                        on the mammoth hive of nest, she may be caught
                            in nervous seesawing turnabouts
                                        and swerves—rival
                                    instincts battling it out
                        within her breast: fear of the too-close
                                        faint man scent
                and compulsion to drop grub into upturned beak.
                        The frantic monkey squirms & wails,
                            while her expectant offspring
                                    below thrills

at the feeding prospect—its gullet
        churning with croaks
            and gurgles of pre-gorging. In that pause,
                that odd to-and-fro hovering
                of wary mother frozen in mid swoop—again and again—
        above her nest, a whole throng of arrows seem to fly

                                    at once, rising
                            from ten or more hidden
                        earth sites, the dugouts arranged

in a semi-circle. A first shaft whizzes
harmlessly between tail feathers, second arrow
pierces mere wingtip, but fatal third
shot fired zings
through the lower neck arc
just above the breast bone . . . The scouts
soon recover
the fallen majesty drooped across her nest rim.
They must carry home the claws, severed
back to the upper leg-joint . . .
proof of slaying.

POSSUM

Roadkill. *Fresh* roadkill.
Cecil slams on the brake, and reverses—too quickly,
I fear—back down curvy ascent
of highway to get a better look. No skunk,
says he. Just a big possum . . . *face twisted awry, legs
smeared into blacktop,
wide pear-shaped belly still intact . . .*
He parks at roadside, unpeels the carcass with his big boot-toe
and whips the puffed torso

over his shoulder,
the long tail wrapped about two fingers like so much
kite string, then swiftly waves
the possum round and round over his head—
whereby to build sufficient torque to fling it a distance
over the road edge
into some far ravine. He would spare
the next driver a possible hair-raising skid into the ditch
to avoid the foamy hulk.

True, it's a hazardous
upswing of road, and maybe he averts a mishap or two,
but Cecil is showing off.
He needn't hurl the possum so far. He wants me
to get a taste of his *wicked pitching arm.* All life's
a show. Sweet chances
to perform with surprise relish
he never forsakes . . . Barrel-bellied and wiry, at once, Cecil's
himself an odd possum

of a man in his way.
But he has no love for a *pouchy woods-rat,* which feeds

on worms, snakes, and maggoty
       rotting vermin—*a cross between a weasel*
             and a pig. Out of control! When a possum gets working on
                   a big game tusked-boar
                         carcass, it keeps gnawing & munching
       until it seems to billow out to nearly twice its belly girth
             like a giant pufferfish.

             And after repeated
       spasms and heaves of vomiting, it'll start in again
like a starving creature, who
       hasn't eaten for weeks . . . Cecil's older buddy
             Jake, age sixty-five, craves possum beyond all else to eat.
             He coaxes his good pal
                   Cecil to gather up heaps of roadkill
       possum, whenever he drives his frequent cross-country taxi gigs,
             and salvage the hoard

             for Jake. But Cecil fears
       that his friend will poison himself, and so he refuses
to support this *grisly habit.*
       Even fresh-caught possum tastes foul to Cecil,
             it eats so much spoiled flesh: it's belly *a putrid cesspool,*
             a garbage dump with claws
                   and slimy tail. He argues with Jake,
       give up this habit quick, before you pollute your blood & brains
             past remedy. How cure

             blood poisoning? Chop
       off the pus-swoll'd member. But possum shall putrefy
your tongue & eyeballs . . . Head
       gangrene . . . Brain rot . . . You can't save a man's life
             by decapitation, dig? . . . But Jake's himself a big arguer,
                   an irascible cuss, who
                         mutters he can always detect—

by simply whiffing a gouge in backside flesh—whether the meat
has begun to spoil. Unless

the possum's *hiney* itself
has turned maggoty or worm-infested, it's safe to eat.
When his hunterly luck is good,
he gorges himself with seven or eight possums
per day, and never has a tummyache, nor spits up bilious
gunk—no sour gas puffing
out of him at either *pipe outlet.*
But from week to week, says Cecil, Jake's paunch balloons out
whole inches. He can see

big jumps at a glance,
and keeps warning Jake to no avail. None of his clothes
can hold him in check: he bulges
and rips every seam . . . Jake snickers. *You too plump*
yourself, Cecil. And you go to fat on beer. So what's obese?
Cecil's no vegetarian,
he'd have me know. On Holiday,
or directly after Sunday Morning Mass, he loves to go hunting,
but spurns possum; rather,

he tracks agouti-rabbit
and wildcat. The lynxes are devilish hard to bring down,
whether by snare or by rifle
shot. Both agouti and cat, favorite game food,
are clean animals, fussy about what they eat: their flesh
always tastes mellow, if tart,
reflecting their own diet. He's sure
he could pass a blindfold test, as regards which local critter
he tastes: *flavor's one thing,*

but wholesome's another. . . .
Ladies too, same blindfold! But in love, he's partial

to all varieties. If pressed,
    he admits he goes sweet quicker for Carib gals—
        who always play hard to get. *And don't you know,* swears he,
            they're still saying, Stop,
                please stop, when they freely strip off
    their own panties for you. He loves best the chancy mood shifts,
        surprise detours & cutbacks

    of the chase, far beyond
        the conquests. Strictly one-night-stands. No romance
between a Black male taxi driver
    like himself and a Carib lass ever goes public,
        so how can it last? He has four regular sweethearts just now,
            he reports: six kids by them,
                two more on the way. *(Not a bad score,*
    yes?, for a man thirty nine.) Two thriving businesses. Taxi squad
        of four drivers, plus rental

    car agency he'd begun
        just last year on taxi profits. No, never been married.
And never wants to be. Divorce
    is fraught with snares and obstacles in Dominica:
        a divorcee is a social leper—stained beyond help, her rep
            permanently smudged. No man
                will give her a tumble. The only worse
    disgrace is AIDS. Does he stand by his gals, through thick & thin,
        or ditch them for petty cause? . . .

    One avidity in life
        he can't control, he divulges, is his gut-craving
for cat meat. Just last year,
    after weeks of failed hunts for his firstlove,
        wildcat, he grew restless and slovenly. His two best pals,
            weary of his heartsickness,
                taunted him to slaughter his mistress

Annie's pet cat; and what had begun as mere jest, teasing, grew
                    into an eerie temptation

                    that invaded his dreams . . .
          One day when Annie was detained at work, he abducted
and drowned her cat in the river,
          barbecued and eaten before she returned home.
          He cooked up an alibi: the cat absconded into the woods.
              She bought it. But for months,
                         she'd wake in the night calling *puss,*
 O puss, where are you, please come back to me. With never a lapse,
              she hopelessly whined & groaned

                    for her runaway kitty.
          Cecil's shame grew so strong, it drove him to malaise
of ennui and self-deflation.
          If he could admit his guilt, it might ease
              the way to a healing catharsis between them. But he lacked
              nerve to clear the air—which clogged
                         in his bronchial tubes, giving him asthma.
 Whenever she mourned the cat, it choked him up . . . He dumped her,
              would never take her back.

PURGATORIO

I snap awake
from brief nap on shipboard—my seat
near the steady drone and grind of motors.
The White Noise lulled me, my notebook fallen to the deck
from my lap as I nodded off . . .
But I *come to,* startled by a bright staticky chorus of faint sounds
floating above the engine hum
and sea-slaps on the hull. I focus my hearing—
shift to the upper
register, and soon I can make out hundreds of squeaks:
tiny insects,
or maybe crickets? But solo chirps
seem to rise above the pack, at intervals,
wholly distinct from rusty engine scrapings. No machines,
these life toots, no mistaking
them for piston steel or cast iron . . .
I give a closer listen.
Discrete bird cheeps sally forth!
I drop to the deck, and begin hunting the source
on all fours—draw
near, and there in a corner nestled beside the ship-
engine's boiler,

two wide low cardboard
cartons are laid out flat upon the floor, one hard-by the other.
Conspicuously, nothing bulks on top of either box,
for all the limited floor space they usurp. Shaped like widely-
expanded egg holders,

both thin cartons
are dotted with many small breath holes.
O numberless scads of whitish baby chicks

are crammed inside, many visibly pushing their yellow beaks
and round whiskery faces
into the air slots. And now I can sense the strongest vibrations,
a ripply wavelike churn,
shuddering the boxes from within: all throats
warbling together,
all those tiny hearts pumping away, till I find myself
amazed—puzzling over
how the cheap pasteboard bins stay intact!
The whirling motion of so many fluttery—
if near weightless—bird wrigglers seems powerful enough to shatter
those cartons apart. Small cracks
do show across the tops. And indeed, three wildly energized chicks
persist in their pecks & clawings
until they've poked their heads through the narrow
air slits, bursting
open a few headsize portholes. Or is it the stampede
and crush of birdy

brethren that has rammed
those wrinkly faces and bulb-heads through the box sides, gaps
not large enough to give access for any whole bird
to pop out of the cramped lockup. I look away, look back again
for a fresh glimpse.

One tiny chick
is squirming so fiercely, it appears
as if he may soon grind his puffed-up
featherpouch of belly clear through the carton's sheath:
his popeyed cottonball skull
writhes this way and that, struggling to cut loose from its neck-
leash & ruffly white torso,
a ball-and-chain to his venturesome braincase.
Meanwhile, a pair

of poked-through heads are stock still, utterly frozen
in place . . .
I see
they've crudely strangulated themselves,
their necks too sharply constricted
in the cardboard wall-holes turned noose. And there's yet another
wee chick, so active and quivery,
boring its face-ram into an aperture. This pilgrim explorer, too,
seems hellbent to snuff out
its brief life. . . .

FERN HEAVEN

(Mt. Scenery, Saba)

Dodging razor sharp vines and shoots, which dangle and loop
across our path, I trip,
       misstep askew, and then find
a raw zigzag
slice has been taken in my forearm by I know not
       what species of tilted
long sawtooth branch starting up from the very pathside
earth itself, and curling downwards
   at a thirty degree angle to our approach,
   teaching me (too late, alas!)
to gravitate

   toward a guessed path centerline, so avoiding the hazardous
               edges. You glance my arm's
      slash up and down, oozing light
             fineline blood
    trickles—leaks from near invisible paper cuts?—
      running from my elbow
  to my wrist, as if seamstress took a quick cross weave
      of stitches through my epidermis
    with her outdoor Singer sewing machine:
      short zigzags back and forth,
           a little trail

of serums illumining the telltale path of her needlework.
Hacksaw Ferns, you declare—
   the weapons, by now, far behind
us on the track.
I've rarely known saw leaves to take so precision
    clean a bite, you say,
fascinated by the decorative network of my bloodlines.

This is my arm hurting, not some lace
    ornament trim sample, I mildly complain.
        But ignoring my retort,
you've launched

        into your first of many freewheeling plant fantasias, brief
                    zippy lectures, improvised
                as we trot, and displaying
                        modest genius
            for transmitting observed data as condensed
                verbal nuggets spewn forth
            on the fly: *more diverse filial rarities in the world*
                    family of ferns peep at humans
                scouting this trail than any island site
                    I've seen . . . We pause to inspect
                        a few hacksaw

spears of fern, waist high, poking serrated frond tips at us
from below, waving their rows
        of razor-fine teeth, menacingly,
at our bare legs,
arms and necks. Set further back in forest, you note
            head-high stalks of Bracken
Fern, taller than your blonde children who keep marveling
at their pliant stems when they tug them
        playfully down to earth, watch them spring back
        like supple rubber-necked
tall sunflowers.

    These high Brackens wield no sharp-edged cutlass at fingers
                    or palms. But your adored
                grandsire in the happy family
                        of Sabian ferns
            is the giant Tree Fern: you point to mammoth fronds
                towering up above, and yes,

the ferns *are* true whole trees, not just huge parasites
vine-yoked to tree upper trunks.
I'm still dizzied from surveying a canopy
of fern web sweeps arched high
overhead,

when you—by abrupt impulse—kneel and bid me stoop, in like
fashion, to minutely peruse
mossy rock at our feet; thereon,
I can make out
some five distinct plantlets, each silhouetted
with finely chiseled snow-
flake edges, fern leaf borders nuzzled up to the moss rims.
These tiniest ferns, almost transparent,
unicellular, are mated to the ever-damp moss
for life fluids, no root system
to store water. . . .

And I pray I may be christened Gulliver of the fern heavens,
a firmament of one-cell-thick
mites lolling beside immense fern
timbers: flora clan
stratified from lowliest earth-filmy thin flakes
underfoot, the hideaway
fern sleepers, to fork-limbed, thick-barked lofty trunks
towering out of sight. Giant Tree Ferns,
your favorite lives on Saba, *grow ever higher,*
broader, denser—as we travel
ever skywards.

III.

TO MERGE WITH TREES

After three hours
    of search for my old friend Nolly,
        I abandon the site of his hilltop house (it looks
    deserted: perhaps he's moved),
and give up the hunt . . . But a wraith leaps
    between two clumps of lush trees into the clearing
        below my footpath: phantom shadow
           of a tall man
              wearing a khaki suit blent, eerily,
                to arboreal
              backdrop—splotchy flower pattern, that Cuban
    guerrilla fashion of the Sixties;
        a few twiggy leaf

sprigs are braided
    around his shirt collar, beltless
        waist, trousers cuffs . . . His camouflage is aided
by a loping sideways shuffle.
One moment, he's a deer risen on both
    hind legs; the next, near-still, a low pinetree
        quivering in the wind. But now
           he sweeps fast
              from woods margin, arms outspread
                to greet me!
              Incognito unpeels from him like a molted
    snakeskin. For two days, one night,
        he's been holed up

in dense woods.
    In hiding? I ask. *Why, otherwise,*
        work so hard to be invisible, to merge with trees,
    ivies and the long grasses.

An elusive woods wraith . . . No reply.
He holds up two empty small matchboxes, shaking
them out to show me they're vacant.
These must carry
the secret of his mission, his work
in the wilds.
Tree farms, he says. *I'm a planter of trees.*
A side of his genius I'd missed
before. Pops open

a third matchbox
delved from a deep key pocket sunk
in his faded Levis. Seeds. Pauie seeds. Piled
to the top, brimful. In autumn
between hard rains, whenever the Bequia
weather's prime moist gasp rises to a new peak,
he'll embark on his next widescale
planterly frolic.
Impregnating the loams, he says.
Today, frangipanis
were his tillage, his delicate prickings
of the turf with his homemade tree-
planter implement,

halfway between
a syringe and a hypodermic. Seed
after seed, ever one by one, his slow innoculations
of earth husk. He stakes out
acres recently despoiled of prime forest
by a medley of sneakthieves: furniture makers and ship
builders, rude campers hacking
the young boles
for their campfires. And gross vandals'
sly depletions
of thriving high timbers. His passion: to *grow*

back, grow back, the stumpy acreage—he's
an unseen tree birth

Czar of the night.
No lawbreaker, he, no transgressor
of forester's or game warden's edict . . . But Nolly
carries out his sorties, his tree seed
rampages, on the sly. They're his sacred rage:
a fury to re-flower the wild hillslopes—blossoming
trees, ever his favorite strains,
breeds, species . . .
He would put back the tall high-flying
blooms and resurrect
the lost mid-island tree groves of his youth.
O let those blossoms fly once more,
ringing Bequia's valley

with petal storms
as thickly splurging as California's
wild poppy fields . . . His impulse to replant the isle's
many blank zones, all tree-denuded
esplanades, knows no bounds. Of late, he fears
that his urge to imbed great seed clusters on private
estate grounds may outrage some land
owners. So far,
most smile upon his antics, even cheer
the newly-sprouted
saplings, that slow upreach of limb and branch.
A windfall. Or free-of-charge boon.
They'd gladly pay fees

for the fly-by-night
secret gardener . . . It could be elves,
or a whole clan of beneficent pranksters, the happy
tree growers. Since artful Nolly's

never been spotted in the act of boring tiny
	grooves for seed, or sprinkling his little cascades
		of fertilizer with salt shakers
			on nipplelike
				puffs in seed beds, who can say whether
					the hit-and-run Tree
				Saint is one compulsive seed hustler, or a team.
			Whoever the breeders, the trees' poorish
				survival rate's no more

than ten per cent
	of any bulk crops planted, no matter
		how much follow-up care and nurturing is pursued.
	Twice a week, Nolly makes the rounds
of his dozens of tree patches, scattered—here
	and there—across the island, spaced out evenly
			from shore to shore. On average,
		a mere fraction
			of the bud-laden saplings manage to grow
				to a six foot height
				putting them well out of range of the scavengers:
			wild goats, donkeys & sheep, all insatiable
				nibblers and munchers

who slash the tops
	off most frail trees before they peak
		into a first-bloom flowering season. They gobble up
	the early buds like so many cherries,
figs, apricots—a succulent treat those wildlife
	cruisers cannot resist. *Nipped, O nipped in the bud!* . . .
		Often, he catches goats in the act
			of cropping trees
				and scoots them away. *It's no use—they'll*
					nail ninety per cent,

        or so, regardless . . . Now he leads me to an orchard
            of young pauie and poinsettia trees
                arranged in a dense

crosshatched pattern.
        In proud full bloom today, all yellow
            and red blossoms are flying high—row by flourishing
        row of the brood raised safely beyond
the reach of those toothy loppers. *Ah, your secret*
        tree farms, I say . . . Next week, when the poinsettias
            mature, he'll be poised beneath
                pistils and stamens
                    to gather the first seed harvest in matchbox
                        incubator—I picture him
                        tapping the pods, spilling a fine spray in his palmed
            repository, braced to plot out his Eden
                of future planting sprees. . . .

THE WARRIOR PRIESTESS

(Port-au-Prince, Haiti)

Twice daily, early and late,
we exit the Chateau—pass through the front gate, and zigzag
    our two-mile stroll downhill to meet Rue Duvalier,
        main artery through Town Center . . .
As always, we're waylaid by hawkers of diverse wares,

                        none so bullying as those Voodoo Scouts,
                            whose graphic accounts
                        of the basic rites and deviltries
                            shall not fail to spark
                                our fantasies'
                        short fuse—their procurer
                    tongues so skilled in arts of purply
                    scene-painting, we'd fast succumb
                            but for mentor Stella's
                                cool warning:
                    Voodoo for tourists is shot through
                        with specious trappings
                    & trumpery—it's devoid of all true magic!

    If we but bide our time, she vows,
she'll ferret out the place and hour for Grande Dame Viola's
    next voodoo *bash*, then smuggle us into adjacent
        hideaway nook of forest,
we to be her mum stowaways, she our renegade

                        chaperone . . . Daybreak finds us hastening
                            down a maze of wooded
                        paths & garden byways, soon installed
                            behind a dense ringside hedge
                                of low shrubs

that both conceal our persons
and afford a full panoramic lookout
on the mid-forest clearing: we
nestle in our squatters'
vantage, hardly
breathing, and partake of deep hush.
A spell. Steadfast vigil
of a hundred-odd assembled rapt-eyed ranks

of gowned and much bejeweled
Nationals. They are mostly women, fair mix of young and old,
and a scattering of men (a few men disguised,
perhaps, as kerchiefed & bonneted
matrons): most folks are half-seated on their knees, bent

forward at the waist, all visibly waiting
out the grand surprise
arrival of the Head Matriarch,
herself. All perfectly
silent, none
seems to know the exact time
for her debut, nor style or direction
she'll choose. Viola takes utmost
pains to improvise, ever,
new openers.
Having a true flair for theater, she'd
keep her flocks guessing.
Today her dizzying approach is heralded

by three yodeled shrieks, mixed
with animal snorts and neighs, each markedly nearer the crowd.
A headlong racing advance from the Southeast
shocks the whole gallery to its feet
at once, facing the sector of her long-held wails. Hordes

swiftly milling about, closed ranks open up
leaving, at the last,
a wedge-shaped fissure between them.
One moment, I notice two rows
neatly aligned
into a V. Then she bursts
upon the rift, galloping at great speed—
borne up high, higher, highest,
she stands fully erect
in the stirrups
of a grand White Stallion whinnying
madly with the pain
gouged by her battering spurs, deeply scored

into the creature's blood-speckled
flanks . . . Plunging toward a fearful cluster of devotees stooped,
transfixed, at the gap's far end, she hauls back
the reins with fiery snap of wrists—
the stallion's hectic dash broken, his bulk weight upswung

& crumpling on his rear heels, both forelegs
raised high, ever higher,
the wild horsewoman towering upright
above the saddle, all eyes
fast riveted
to her face—the spectators
ravished, as well, by her flamboyant
costume: that antique uniform
of ex-dictator Papa
Doc's cavalry.
Flaming red tights & riding britches.
Red, gold-buttoned jacket.
Glary red helmet topped with a great furled

ostrich feather, aquiver. Scarlet
neck kerchief. For contrast, those sparkling black boots, black
police gloves . . . Her thick right glove tugging reins
taut near the breaking point, left hand—
ungloved now—sweeps back over her shoulder and snatches

from an unseen pouch a wild fluttery thing
of squawks & croaks, snowing
white feathers into the sea of faces
below the horse's upraised
thin front hoofs.
Without pause, she now stuffs
the live rooster's head into her mouth—
yellow beak, red comb & wattles
all squeezed and compacted
within her puffed-
out cheeks. Then clamping the palpitant
neck with her front teeth,
she grasps both legs and yanks stubby tail

outwards, while jerking her helmeted
jaws from side to side: two twists severing the neck cord.
She spits out the decapitated bulb, wattled
silhouette twirling like a rose
or red-petaled pinwheel over the crowd, and she swings

the white headless trunk in widening circles,
streams of blood spattered
in all directions, most faces staring
upward at the blood storm
in motionless
ecstasy. A few youths, loudly
chanting, run to and fro—they all chase
rain of droplets, hoping to catch
squirts & globules of blood

to thickly smear
on their cheeks and foreheads like gobs
of Indian Warpaint. At last
she dismounts, and unsheathing a silver knife

from her belt holster, slashes open
horizontal gouges in a canvas saddlebag: a wobbly live bulk
slides through the gash, dropping to the earth
at her feet, taking one bounce
on its back—a loud thud. The goat scrabbles in the dirt

for a footing, but she kicks its tawny butt
downward and pins him close
with her bare knee, red riding britches
bunched in a tourniquet loop
around her thigh.
She beckons to an expectant
tall figure, a bronze-skinned woman, hale
and long-boned like herself,
who advances swiftly
to the inner
circle drawing behind her by the wrist
a second light-footed
personage of short stature, head concealed

in canvas bag. At the last moment,
that guide lady gently nudges her small charge toward Viola
murmuring soft blandishments and backs away—
the hooded figure takes small steps,
pauses (many low voices, behind, coax her to proceed):

ever so hesitantly, she resumes blind hobble
pace and finds herself
stumbling into Viola's clasp. She falls
to her knees, cowers and moans

with terror. Spasms
ripple across her back and limbs.
Her breath comes in heaves. Tall Priestess
snatches the hood from the convulsive
child's face (revealed at last
to be a girl
of no more than twelve years), raises
shiny knife overhead,
and plunges it into the pinned goat's abdomen,

while we struggle to suppress our gasps,
fearing the child herself shall be next victim of the carnage.
So much blood's spurting into the damsel's hair
and face, we're dumbfounded! *O where
has the knife struck? Whose blood is spilled?* . . . But Viola

has now ripped the goat's heart—still pumping
madly away—from its breast.
And she holds the pulsating dark organ
over the hysterical child's head
and squeezes,
wringing the heart's contents
from its chambers like a laundress expelling
last squirts from an inert sponge.
Dropping the shrunk flesh-
melon, she grasps
the girl roughly under both arms, lifts
her from bent-kneed squat
to her feet, and commences spinning the waif

like a top; whereupon a perky troop
of five young women spring forward from the rows of seated
or upright spectators and, with the panache
akin to veteran cohorts of Black
Magic, they resume the task of whirling the child.

Passing her back and forth between them, they
massage and caress her limbs
by turns, inducing upon her limp frame
the frenetic gyrations
of a *danse*
macabre; and soon, she starts
to pick up the moves on her own, ensemble
of helpers falling away, one
by one, dance now fully
autonomous
and rapt, a breathlessly fast sweep,
twirl and wheeling about:
a *Soul Possessed.* Her spins become so rapid

she seems to blur before our eyes,
a human gyroscope . . . After a measured pause, the Warrior
Priestess steps back into the charmed circle,
the child's dance winding counter-
clockwise around the dead goat carcass. Viola raises

her hands and claps loudly twice, the dancer's
whirligig and turnabout
frozen in mid-stride. She faints, limbs
folding up beneath her, while
unseen chorus
of hummer voices and soft drumbeats
cease. Viola waves her hands over the fallen
(now comatose) child, as if wafting
away lethal ill spirits.
One-and-all
present, ourselves included, feel her
Giving up the Ghost
of deathly ague, now peaceful sleep welling up. . . .

THE SHE BABE

We drive to a secluded shore, where rough waters
and surf constantly pound the rock-
studded beach: none dare swim
here—the undertow
is treacherous in any weather. Years back
many folks drowned
who were fooled by rare surface calm,
no few champion
swimmers among them. This rugged
stretch of coast—

kept secret from visitors
and tourists—is the setting for Franz Booi's film script, based
on the true story of a young girl, no more than twelve
years old, whose father was abducted by a team of pirates midway
in a fishing excursion begun

in these offshore waters. Fair-haired Appolonia,
guessing she was the prime target
of the attack, discovered
that swift ambush
in time to leap overboard (her father, alas,
too preoccupied
with dragging his mackerel-laden
nets over the side rail
to notice the sneak advance—
low paddle boat

quietly streaking out
between two high reefs that gave them cover till the last moment);
a marvelous swimmer, child wonder who learned to swim

before she could walk, Appolonia sped away underwater, circled
behind the invader trio

and clung to the underedge of a low coral reef
before hiddenly surfacing for air
some minutes later. Father
was now blindfolded
& tortured before her eyes, in futile hope
that his howls would
lure her forth from hideaway nook
for capture. They tied
his arms and legs with ropes,
then slowly tore

his ligaments & muscles
with a stretching wheel—no show! She kept her distance, unwavery,
though they rent him limb from limb. She'd seen how men
could mortify and desecrate the flesh of a fellow human, and she
gave up on the whole Race

of mortals on the spot, thereafter taking a vow
to throw herself upon the wayward
mercy of the elements
and to forsake
all succor of human society—whether dear
kinsfolk or friend . . .
She quickly garnered a balanced cuisine
of algae and sea kelp
scoured with blunt shell-tools
from the undersides

of shallow rocks and coral,
which gave her ample nutriment. For years, she but rarely ventured
ashore to sample land flora and vegetation, surviving
mostly in peninsular caves—those facing away from all landlocked
territory; if she emerged

by day, she slithered through deep coast gullies
that connected by tunnels & sinkholes
with undersea grottoes.
She came to know
the circuit of interlacing land and sea
caverns as if she,
herself, were amphibious creature—
a mermaid or seasnake
with arms who had memorized,
perfectly, the map

of all underwater escape
routes. At long last, in her late teens she grew reckless, often
popping out to sun herself voluptuously on reef-tops
within easy viewing of this remote shorescape overlooking the site
of her horrid banishment.

Long since forgotten and presumed dead, the *She
Babe* had faded from public memory (as did
her father, whose dismembered
carcass washed ashore,
piecemeal) . . . One day, a crew of workmen—
building a massive
oil refinery on that headland
jutting high above
her usual sunbathing reef
haunts—spotted her.

They were driven wild
with fever at sight of long-limbed sleek-skinned Appolonia, hair
grown down past her knees, naked except for anklets,
bracelets, and necklace of seaweed she'd woven into clever designs
for her amusement: patterns

based on sailor's bowknot, slipknot, half hitch
that her seafaring daddy had taught her.

Perhaps the lacework of vine-
jewel ringlets
she wore were a tribute to her glad papa's
memory. What else
did she have to remember him by? . . .
Word spread. The droves
of men and a few young boys—
Franz was one,

age thirteen—hung out
in late afternoons. Hidden behind rocks on cliff-top impending
over her roost, they lined up to take their turn, each
so quiet you could hear distant cheeps of shorebirds. The *She Babe,*
strangely, never noticed

the constant band of oglers filing past an ideal
peep hole . . . Once at daybreak, two seamen
sped towards her rowing a silent
paddleboat, whether
to get a closer look or lay hands on her;
but at their nearest
approach, she slipped away so fast—
sleek as a sea otter
or walrus—they never saw her
flick the water,

but found in her place
a tiny whirlpool where she sank. After that near miss, she vanished
for months, then would reappear at uncertain intervals.
Franz had seen her only twice, but his puberty was haunted by dim
flashback to her luminous

wavy gold hair, loosely fallen across the small
of her back and hips—it seemed to flow
down to her ankles . . . Years later,

it was rumored
that she came inland on darkest nights (no
moonlight or stars)—
to take a lover, that ignorant boorish
halfwit: the goatboy!
Those lucky few who caught sight
of them, flailing

on spongy turf, declare
that they grunted & shrieked during coitus like wild mountain cats.
And one night three shepherds plotted a surprise pounce,
concealed behind a dense patch of cactus near that usual trysting
place, until they sprang

from cover at mid-coupling and lassoed her
with rope snares flung from diverse
angles: they displayed wrist-
snap and swagger
like cowboys entrapping a wild runaway
stallion, tossed a fish
net over her head, then wrapped her
in tarpaper & lugged
her back to town. Soon after,
she was coerced

to accept Holy Communion
from the Priest in Rincon . . . Slowly, she grew to be *half-civilized,*
but resumed secret flings with her goatherd beau. Tame or
wild, Appolonia lived a long life, outlasting all those who swaddled
& bagged her in from the sea.

ETHER

Ether days . . .
Back in late Forties
St. Maarten, teen-age Tony Hodge—
wiry and keen-eyed, a kid with lizard's
reflexes—was hired as the surgical assistant.
Wound dresser. Apprentice to fledgling
male nurse, Tony
bustled from hemorrhaging
bleeder to just-cauterized amputee
in makeshift
clinics: no Full Service Hospital in those days,
just an open deck ward strung out
along the beach, comprised
of a dozen

flat cots, stand-ins for real beds . . .
He scampered to and fro between the afflicted
like a budding Jimmy Cagney.
Once he twisted
a tourniquet around small child's
leg artery aspurt, held a firm gauzeball
plug to a woman's punctured neck and strapped dimestore
adhesive tape in place with his free hand, all

in a single
balletic dance motion.
They were so short-handed, he had
to whirl his brisk pirouettes from cot
to bench to displaced and recycled bar stools,
mastering the chores of three adept
nurses in today's
emergency wards. Dependable

beyond measure he was, often piloting
speedy horse-
drawn flat-cart ambulance from traffic mishaps,
piling some half-a-dozen or more
injured bods like sardines
on bargelike

low cart decks, and strapping them
side-by-side with wide leather thongs or criss-
crossing bungee cords. And once,
in a mad rush
following an accident, he strapped
two blood-gusher limbs together to quick-plug
the wounds; by all accounts, he saved both lives, the man's
leg clamped to the adjacent woman's arm, stanching

all blood spills,
the two slender victims
stacked head-to-foot, foot-to-head,
to get their limbs lined up for mutual
counter seal . . . But Tony's foremost job detail,
as surgeon's assist, was dispensing
KNOCKOUT DROPS.
His touch with the ether bottle
was near flawless—no one else of whatever
age or gender
could be trusted to dribble ether sprinklings
with his finesse and adroit control.
Five or six whole droplets
could put under

the brawniest longshoreman, say,
for a specified expanse of minutes—near uncanny,
his knack for fitting the dose
to exact size

of the wound and mass of the pre-
amputee. The youth had a perfect instinct
for anesthesiology! . . . *Count backwards from one hundred
to one,* he'd murmur, as he pattered those tiny

slow drips down—
nobody lasted past ninety
five, that seventh drop "overdose"
always held in check. Afterwards, when
he kept vigil, he'd positively know an eyelid's
tremor, a nervous tic or muscle twinge
from true wakeup
signal—provided he could keep
an eye on the patient. If not, not. Tony
was underage,
after all, and held subject to police-enforced
restrictions. He must stand behind
a broad translucent screen,
his ether flask

at the ready, while his mentor
physician—a G.P. who dabbled in all health
crises, from gout to scooping
out brain tumors—
set the compound fractures, fast-
sewed long stab wounds like a tailor stitching
a trousers cuff or shirt seam, reattached severed members
and rebuilt crushed hand or foot, threading digit

after digit,
joint by joint . . . Yes, Tony's
chief role, drilled daily, was to wait,
wait in patience behind the shade (common
civility or politeness forbade *juvenile* viewing
of nudity); he would scan the lit-up

screen for clues.
If an arm or leg silhouette
shot out at weird angles, our Tony knew
he'd be summoned
for booster dose—*pump him up again, Ether Boy*—
and he gave his least trickle of drops,
teen junkie poised to deliver
the next fix.

CACTUS LOVE

I.

For hundreds of years,
Arubian houses
have been guarded
by tall Cadushi cactus
fences. And even today
old plantation manors
turned private estates

                     keep up
                     the long-lived
                     belts
                     of prickly
                     fence posts,
                     sturdy as
                     our cyclone fences,
                     more forbidding
                     to intruders
                     than barbed wire.

How long
do the separate cacti
fence posts live?
How often
replaced, freshly planted?

                     They seem poised
                to outlast all homes they've engirded, or
                the few cycles of family
                ensconced within . . . We are left

pondering cacti as barriers,
grim thorn poles to repulse the visitor—
little do we guess
the beauty and fecundity of this phylum,
        this hardy tribe. . . .

Julio Maduro,
a lover of cactus, cheers
the brute survivorship
of Aruba's 48 wild species
            of cacti. Julio, himself, first
            identified and named
                two or three rarities, always
                on the lookout
for yet another new hybrid to add
to the bristly roster. Most are night-
bloomers, he tells me, so you must
venture out on a moonlit eve
to best view

                    the glittery array
                    of cactus flowers and fruit.
                    A mere trio bloom
            by day, two species are bloomless,
            and two more—one by day,
            the other by night—produce edible fruit.

                    And so saying, he shuffles
                    in midstroll,
                        veers sideways from our path
            to pluck
a small greenish pod from a half-
hidden recess
                    in a low forked cactus, bursts
                    the thin shell with thumb
                    and forefinger,

then offers me
a taste of the succulent morsel,
a cross between kiwi
and apricot—to my palate.

            Local naturalists and gardeners,
            like Julio, crave range
            of types, unwilling to settle
            for the native 50-odd
            cactus varieties,

                        who keep importing
                        more and more bulbs, slips, cuttings
                        from other lands, Arizona mostly,
                        to adorn

        or enhance their exotic gardens.
            At last report, no fewer
than 200 discrete species
of named cacti
were known to populate
                        Aruba's private and public
                        arboretums, parks or home plots. . . .

        2.

                Julio points
            to a few wee squat
                cacti, one by one,
    half-hidden by low branches
            of tall Mesquites
        towering over the Melos,
            as if the miniature
        cacti shrink from sun—

crouching in the shade of upright
timbers. But *No*, says Julio.
They can flourish as well
without or with shadow cover: hardy
bush shapes, prickly bulbs,
they often encircle
the base of those high trunks
by chance—pure caprice
of timing, in all such cases.
For they were here
first, and last,
too, shall they be . . .

Overfond of this breed
he may be—his secret mate among
cactus clans! *How good is your sight?*
asks Julio, drawing
me after him
to an elevated rock plateau stationed
beside tall Cadushi,
its long pipelike serpentine arms
extending 30 or 40 feet above.
He points to the tops
of lower limbs, aquiver at eye level.
Stare close. Closer. What
do you see, Larry?

Is it seed pods,
sprouting thistles that shake
cotton-tail puffballs
in the light afternoon breezes?
The tiny shapes,
poised at right angles
to the bulbous limb ends, flutter.
I can make out wing blurs!

They are tiny birds,
their beaks piercing the cactus

rind—as if sipping nectars
therefrom, disguising their moves
as wind-pulsed sticker pods,
a camouflage to hide
them from hawks, snakes, iguanas,
that host of natural foes
and predators.
                    Now I ask
after odd, twisted shapes,
            driftwood swirls
as of windswept knobs and ruffles,
        topping a few cacti—
anomalies—of no set species,
            any size or age.
        It's a virus, he replies,
that afflicts the plants: tumors
may become elephantine,
dwarfing the victim cactus.
No doubt, they are stricken,
            but slow to die.
                    Julio has a keen eye
                    for longevities. Like doctors,
                    who can pick a soon-to-die human
                    from the ballpark crowd
                    by his pallor, or telltale vesicular
                    bulge, he spots
                    the near-lame cactus oldster.
                    Despite a robust, puffed-out barrel
                    shell, the hardy exterior
                    may soon deflate,
                    wither, and collapse from within.
            Together, we survey
        three tallest cacti. Julio
            knows, at a glance,
which will die soon, which live on

into—maybe beyond—
the 21st Century.
One chest-puffed thick cactus
is ailing, says he: the inflated
trunk betrays inward rot.
He gives it one year's
grace period, two winter seasons
at the outside.
The trunk's pouch will pop, exploded
like an angry blister,
spewing out rot-blackened innards,
then sloping forward
in a hooplike slow death flop.
The side-by-side
twin, for size and class,
though marred with two goiterlike
bluish growths
on top of the main trunk, will survive!
No life-threatening virus,
this common cactus
ailment—from here, it could outlast
two human lifelines.

3.

Julio, at 66, loves to sleep
upon the bare earth. Two to three hours per night's enough!
As he grows older, he needs
less sleep; besides, most heart attacks occur
during sleep (sleep took his two elder brothers, both snuffed out
just before daybreak). . . . Short naps
give death fewer chances
to strike the wary sleeper, who
keeps one eye half-open, trained on the thief's

                                        approach. He beds down
                    late, awakes long before first light & walks
                                        pre-sunrise hours among
                            beloved faces,
                                the blooms of cactus
            flowers: they nod to him and ruffle their petals, he
                            the secret sharer
                            of their starlit—
                    or moonlit—openings. Ah, he may inhale
                            the faint aromas, or pluck
                    a fruit or two,
                                no harm in it, he takes

                his cactus breakfast early. No way
        sleep furies can get him!—his prickly darkling companions,
            tall arms thrust starwards,
                    will take him to their sheltering greeny
        breasts. Lately, in briefest catnaps, he dreams that a maternal
                    Cadushi enfolds him, brushing
            his overnight face bristles
                with her own fluff of whiskers,
                    the flaxen thistle down of her bosom. . . . By day,

                        spry Julio basks
                in his late life's newborn ruggedness.
                            He can roam all day, dawn
                    to dusk, yet take
                    no sips of liquid
            refreshment. He goes off into midsummer desert blaze
                        for prolonged hikes,
                    arduous rock climbs,
                with no canteen, no waterflask; his throat
                        never grows parched, nor breath
                comes short, nor eyes
                        blur. Less water, less

sleep, each day he trains to make do
with less. And he sings to the cactus blooms, he would be
        of like Soul, a Kin to cactus
                    aridities. . . . Julio, I see, looking closer
at his face, neck and ears, is spotted and blemished—bespattered
                    with warts, splotches, small tumors:
those two pendant growths
        hung from his pouchy eyelids
                like tiny chandeliers; the bags under his eyes

                        sporting flat leechlike
        blister lumps; the rim of his left nostril
                    distorted by squarish
            wide globule
                that nearly usurps
    the underlying tissue into its own gross fistula—each
                lesion a tattoo, a mark
            of Arubian nightfall
        metamorphosis. *Staunch cactus man, Julio,*
            you drink the sun & turn
        a cold cheek to
                Karmas of the rain!

THE DIVI-DIVI TREES, FORSAKEN

Bonaire, the Naturalist's Eden, a front-
runner in conservation laws, provides true sanctuary
for over one hundred species
of migratory birds: the famed pink flamingos
that build their mud-pie nests midway in the chain
of commercial salt ponds, some flapping a twilight
flight south to Venezuela

daily; yellow-winged parrots
(*Lora* the rare
local species), indigenous parakeets
and golden
orioles among them. Two broad
regions were granted
Ecological Preserve status in the year
Nineteen Eighty, enforced
by the Dutch Crown.
Washington Slagbaii National Park,
a huge northernmost
quadrant of the island. And Bonaire Marine Park—
the entire coastline of this country,
projected to a two-hundred-foot-deep
offshore harborage

radiating, equidistantly, in all
directions. Other isles have tried to follow Bonaire's
lead in ecological reforms,
but few approach her fervid steadfastness
in enforcing the Law—stiff fines and jail sentences
levied upon the violators . . . Just south of urban
Kralendijk, we pass a nest

of towers, Trans World Radio's
810,000 watt
transmitters, most powerful radio complex
in the Dutch
Isles. It broadcasts *The Vision*
in seven languages
throughout South America and the Caribbean:
Protestant missionary
programs. The vast
worldwide network of radio centers
was founded as Voice
of Tangiers in '54, most recent adjunct stations
proliferated to the Soviet Union,
a June '90 opening of the Leningrad
Mission soon followed

by small-scale transmitters in Kiev & Moscow . . .
My confidante Elena, that expat Italian piano teacher
of some twelve years' Citizen standing
in Bonaire, vents her private gripes with TWR's
local franchise—secretly given privileged status by Dutch
Magistrates, *in league with the American CIA*
she claims. All foreign businesses

begun in Bonaire are granted
ten years tax-free
service, but Trans World's taxless perk seems
perpetual . . .
She reports a recent plague scare,
hushed-up in the local
media: two articles just published in reputed
journals cite statistics
of six times
normal incidence of cancer deaths
for human victims

dwelling near the transmitters (within a three-mile
radius, some rare forms of malignancy
noted, often linked to huge doses of high-
frequency radiation) . . .

Shocking, too, is the upswing in maladies
that have struck prize fauna and flora, islandwide—worst
incidence within closest range
of the transmitters. Two or three rare species
of parakeet dying in record-high numbers, one perhaps
dying out. A few varieties of cactus sprouting
wildly bulbous tumors, often

distorting the familiar tube
shapes of finger
or organ-pipe cacti beyond recognition
before the stalks
cave in upon their own rotted
marrows. And finally,
as local families observe to their chagrin,
epidemic wood cancer appears
to be wreaking
havoc on most of Bonaire's popular
Divi-Divi trees.
Oldtimers, in particular, have begun to sorely pine
over the loss of those beautiful wind-
blown shapes dotting the desert landscape
at regular intervals . . .

To my novice eye, those trees appear to mimic
today's puffed-out bouffant hair styles, varied by original
hairdressers to give a trendy chic
blown-to-one-side permanent wave; these unique trees
seem to display an arboreal incarnation of the ceaselessly

gusting trade winds, as if wind waves could gayly evolve
woody shapes, put down roots

                    and shake out branches to freely
                              etch their gaseous
                    personalities . . . O soon to be ravaged,
                                        alas! Even so,
                    the Powers of the Ministry, *wealth-
                              crazed,* turn a deaf ear,
                    while the local government and news media,
                              too, look the other way . . . Months
                                        back, a grass-roots
                              protest group of *Concerned Citizens*
                              marched in the streets
          brandishing skull-and-crossbones posters at oncoming
                    traffic: they urged the installation
                    of protective shields around the power
                    transformers. Lead casings,

          they proposed, would radically cut back
          the surfeit of radiation spewn into the lower atmosphere
without reducing wattage or impeding
          that vast range of Church broadcast. But the debate
          flagged, no action taken . . . Today, it's far riskier for TWR
to appear to admit the least blame—any word of safety
devices is quickly squelched.

DUELING U-BOATS: BONAIRE, 1944

To this day business partners in Oil,
Holland and America jointly ran the Bopek oil storage
and refinery complex. Monthly,
huge supertankers would unload the barrels
of fresh crude shipped from Africa and the Middle East,
to be refined and stored briefly in Bonaire,
then transferred to small tankers

headed for the States . . . In 1944,
Eleanor Roosevelt disembarked for a surprise week-long
visit to Bonaire, she and FDR
held in highest esteem throughout the ABC
islands. Her *stopover,* greatly lauded in the media,
drew attention away from the high casualty
list of native fishermen

slain, recently, by German Sub attacks
on local fishboats—all craft suspected of espionage.
True, Bonaire's U.S. Marine base
was the largest in the area. Strong radar
signals had tipped off cruising Subs of the Third Reich—
spy activity was heating up; hence, their all-out
Blitzkrieg on commercial sea

vessels of every size and class,
having no way to pinpoint the source of radar units.
The Sub Admirals placed their bets,
supposing the Enemy would be shrewd enough
to hide radar transmitters on civilian fishing sloops
and sailboats, going after these with a vengeance.
Lovely highborn families

were torn apart by the decimation
of *non-combatant males*. Wives begged their mates to stay
off those war-smitten sea lanes . . .
    WEEK ONE. A large warehouse was evacuated,
        stripped of all desks, cabinets. Word leaked out: a dozen
local German families were rounded up, detained
for questioning and herded

        into one room of internment quarters
        for *housekeeping*. WEEK TWO. Three large boatloads arrived—
at ten hour intervals—from Aruba
    and Curacao: full German family contingent
        of those Dutch neighbor isles quickly scuttled by dark
into basement rooms of that same public works
arena turned barracks. For days,

        no clue was forthcoming in the news media
        or public forum. That was the first wave . . . WEEK THREE.
Various non-German folks were summoned
    to court, mostly South Americans and immigrant
        Europeans—they too detained in the one blank stockade,
termed *enemy sympathizers*. Then a second wave
of boatfuls converged on the pre-

        dawn wharf, hurriedly depositing scores
        of inmates, adults and children in near-equal numbers
culled from the Sister States (more
    sympathizers, perhaps?) . . . Friends and distant
        relatives of detainees started a round of public mutterings,
soon warned by police to *put a lid on* their squawks
of protest. Oh, who could fathom

        the numbers forcibly cloistered in make-
        shift detention village, not unlike—so many whispered
in secret—those infamous *Jap*

relocation camps in California and elsewhere
in America? And how could these immigrant ex-German
nationals be in cahoots with the killer Sub
Chiefs, who were marauding local

fisher fleets? . . . Some bereaved families
of German Sub-attack casualties, taking vague solace
from that queer retaliation against
the aggressors' countryfolk, sought to muzzle
all critics of the mass jailings. Months passed. Finally,
well over a hundred POWs were confined
to the compound, which sprawled

to include a tented courtyard. Rumors
began to circulate—both on radar and in the town square
marketplace—that two large fishing
vessels, as yet undamaged, were conscripted
by the Dutch Crown to carry food and medical supplies
for the German hostages and the burgeoning
flock of *Ethnic Allies,* comrades

in the spirit. If either of those *Mercy
Schooners,* seafaring ambulances, were sunk by submarine
torpedos, so be it! No other boats
would take their place. Marked with Red Cross
Logos, the hospital ships were left unscathed. In ensuing
weeks, all bombings and underwater shellings of area
craft had dwindled to zero. . . .

IV.

EPITAPH TO A WATERING HOLE

(Phillipsburg, St. Maarten)

I keep circling the old haunts, maybe I mis-
        judged the short distance
from beachfront road's dead end
        to that favorite hideaway
                meeting place
            of oldtimers, insiders,
    & Spanish half-breeds. O what's become
        of the shore Bar Espanola? . . .
            No use. Torn down last
                fall, says Tony,
        to build the mall and this suite
            of offices. It's kaput.
Then local charm, in short supply, has taken

a big hit. I shall mourn its passing. *Any word*
                of pretty Marie, I ask?
        The barkeep with the heart-lifting
            smile. Her Spanish greetings
                always soared
        above the racket of billiards,
or those embattled rival dartboard teams
    who play for high stakes, and pitch
        the needle-sharp tailfinned
                missiles—as knife
    throwers might hurl blades—across
        the blindingly smoke dense
indoor arena. The overhead bare bulbs, adangle

from tin chains, swung in the sea gusts, light
        flickering and dimming,
    momentary blackouts quite frequent—

Marie often having to duck
flung darts
as she refilled the players'
beer mugs . . . For two years she was Tony's
right hand at the beer-tap helm:
it about broke his heart
to have to *send*
her packing—sweet little canary who
always had a kind word
for the least of folks, whether local paupers

or transient riffraff. He wept openly the day
he signed her *walking*
papers, while she—of the stiff
upper lip—flashed her
crooked smile,
stroking Tony's left cheek
to comfort *him* . . . Teary-eyed now, he says
it was those welts, hives, blister
lumps on her neck & arms
that left him
no choice. *They swelled and might pop*
or squirt! He'd blinked away
her months of coughing, what with the dozens

of heavy smokers clumped in the rear gallery
hacking their lungs apart.
But those leaky skin pustules
were *over the top*—if
word got out
to the Dutch Ministers,
they'd snap away his rare liquor license
and maybe blacklist him, as well,
till the year two thousand.
Those last weeks

of her headaches, dizzy spells, joint
stiffenings—she laughed
it all off, until the sad day when she winged

up to Montreal for tests. And full-blown HIV
it was. In just two months,
she would choke on her own ruptured
blood spill—the respirator
gave no help
at all. Soon after, a French lad
she'd cottoned to quickly expired. *He* gave
her the killer sting, not the other
way around, folks agreed. Or
so they hoped.
Prayed. Scads of local male fare, teens
to grandsires (a few Chief
Ministers perhaps—but *hushaby,* Tony hoarsens

down to a whisper), quaked in their boots. O
the panic, you could *smell*
fear: it hung in the harbor dawn air
like post-storm fish-belly
rot. Or skunk
roadkill. Nobody uttered
a syllable of the terror, but to this day
the scare's so thick in the misty
beach wind, you can often
hear sucked-in
breaths, muffled gasps, held-down groans . . .
Who kept count of the bevy
of men and boys that she favored after hours?

MOON HOLE

It's a three-quarter-hour stroll across Canoun
to the airstrip, plus six minutes
beyond the runway edge
to the upsweep
in the wooded valley, then abrupt dropoff . . .
No billboards or
signposts point the way—but you can't
miss the landmarks.
Tonight's the one best day
of the month. Start

after dinner, just before
sundown. The twilight pink glimmer on surf and shoreline below
keeps shifting its pale hues as you advance. You know
it's never the same shade twice! All play of faint quarter-tones
eerily portends the misty

dreamscapes of *Moon Hole.* Go now. You must arrive
just at dusk. None of the ghostly
radiance will be lost
on you . . . Head
bowed, I set out at the appointed time—
and it is true,
the gradual efflorescence of scene
unfolds as promised.
When I mount the last steps
of valley rise

a first curved sliver
of light peeks out over dun horizon, the left side of a clown's
tinfoil grin. A fish-hook caught in a high tree

branch, dipped in day-glo-silver paint, but thinner. It's curved
like a white eyelash hair,

O yes, a white floating curled hairline of light.
If I blink at the sickle of ashen
silver, it seems to wink
back. If I grin,
it returns my smile, whitish coiled mouse tail
plastered on the dark.
Or like a first tendril of plantlet
upthreading from loam,
frail moon-slice flares out,
stays, then casts

its slant glow on crater-deep
hollow depression of earth below my stance on the steep verge—
rim of a wide circle. Some five homes oddly shrink
and hunker down in that hollow, each distant from the others,
spaces between them aflicker

and pulsating with waves of moony first light.
New moon birth light. A neon glimmer
swirling all about misty
low slopes of Moon
Hole. It's a magic splash of light! How can
so much light over-
spill emanate from a moon slice
pared so fine? . . . *Look*
closer, I say, to my lupine
eye (howsoever

narrow a skein of moon
shows, the wolf of me springs forth): at opposite faroff poles
of crater's wide maw, two pairs of figures, limbs

intertwined, are nestled beside fallen tree-trunks. Both sets
of snuggling couples lean

into the unearthly pale moon glow, their faces
alit, four little *full* moons of human
skin murmuring and nodding
over the grass.
Every night they come here, old marrieds,
newlyweds, courting
teens. They come from all remote
cays and islets,
far North or South. From all
outflung retreats

and shore coves of Canoun
they converge on this low-lying depression, a carved-out gulley:
natural scoopout of land steeply gouged into coral
terrain like an open-pit mine . . . The earliest traces and flakes
of NEWMOON catch fire

here, this a first mirroring of thin-shaved moon,
sudden cat's-eye wink on the Antilles
Grenadine empyrean, MOON HOLE
always thieving
the best virgin light. And if the ship of love
has run afoul, keel
and hull blistered or mercilessly popped
on shore rocks—down low
in Canoun, sweet light of healing
may begin again.

ACROSS THE STARLIT DUSK

Glad Jonathan
in the lead, we approach
the Isle's two-hundred-sixty foot
summit . . . I've hardly noticed the faint
shifts and altered shadings of oncoming Dusk,
the twilight's gradual upcreep
and linger veiled
by our chatty slow ascent
of the hillslope. We keep pacing
last glimmers
of the fleeting and lowering sun, while half-
dark hauntingly slithers over us
like a molting crumpled
snakeskin. When

at last we mount
the few long terraced steps
over the Apex, a chain of voices
surges all about us . . . Yes, sudden flock
of Canada Geese cackling overhead is surprise
voice weave, as well, whickery gurgles
and hoarse coughs
seeming to trail the feather-
streak flappers by hundreds of yards;
though our ear
absently corrects the wide optical divergence . . .
Or a first chattering of crickets
at nightfall: one early
stutterer touches

off that host
of hundreds into its whir
and fizzle—that's another swift
startup of chorus from the pre-dusk void . . .
But this fluttery whirl of *homebody* voices! Oh
I've never before now heard the like.
Young Jonathan's
figure stalking over the bluff
into full view of the far side lean-tos,
shacks and huts
has stirred a gush of hollers, catcalls, hoots
and chants. Neighbors are warbling
gay tunes to each other;
countless voice

spears are hurled
upon us at once, most folks
blathering over their shoulders
without once turning to face the known
listeners—as if our wide expanse of hillslopes
and valley have shrunk into the One
Family's house
rear. Four or five snatches
of yard mutter may crisscross, interlace,
but no voice
strands ever seem to be getting tangled or mis-
cued. A few gifted vocalists burst
into song, other crooners
soon ringing out

tuneful response.
This interactive medley
of voice and matching counter-
voice is a form of sung repartee blurted
between friends and neighbors. Quarter-mile gaps,

all voice distances traversed,
are swiftly closed . . .
Amazing wide-angled discourse
trills the air! Our telephones, faxes,
and E-mails seem
nullified by this bevy of naked voices, finding
and losing and embracing each
other across the Moonlit
or Starlit Dusk.

ANGEL AT THE HELM

The Kingstown Snapper, legendary mailboat—all
things to all people
like magical *Coat-of-Many-Colors*—
comes chugging into Union
Isle's Harbor.
It's the fabled gateway,
the lucky travelers dispersed over
three deck levels, their eyes
aglitter as they stand
on the verge
of the New Life, the New World.
From downisles & upisles
they come, twice-weekly, on this crowded boat

of many stops,
Ark of many deliveries:
it's their PASSKEY to the Mecca
of Free Port shopping and bartering . . .
This excursion's their best chance of the week,
month, year to enter another
wave of feeling,
a wider scope than home base:
where it's at, so their glistening teeth
& quivery nostrils
bespeak! And I'm riding this wave of new dream
with them, having trudged my way
on unbowed slow sea legs
up the spiral

stairwell, looming upon deck after deck; now I
reach the topmost level,
a tiny circular disc affording

footroom for only three
of us at once.
Teetering three-stories-high
over the traffic-giddy sea lanes, I
survey the incoming yachts,
sail-masted vessels,
and speedboats
beetling around our sluggard course,
zigzagging and crisscrossing
ahead of our prow. We could be standing still.

I check out
the Captain's shrunk upper
quarters adjacent to my roost—
the Great Wheel spins on air, no hand
to guide or control it: sloops and schooners
cutting across our path, but no one
at the steering
post to dodge or outmaneuver
that manic fleet of ships bearing down
on the harbor buoys
reducing them to so many wobbly useless pegs
in the peg board of wild coastal
interchange . . . *Zowee,* I yowl
at the nearest

deckhand. *Nobody's at the helm, we'll crack up,*
what gives? . . . Look again,
says he, *but lower.* I raise myself
on tiptoe, and stare down
at tousled locks
of the towhead poised erect
under the steerage, half as tall or less
from top to toe than the wheel
that he absently plies

with the pinkie
of his left hand, eluding all streams
of harbor cross-traffic
and swerving to skirt many a near miss. Always,

he comes up
smiling after a lethal
close call. *He's the Captain's
ten-year-old son,* the deckmate tells me
with unruffled aplomb. *He navigates these Union
Isle approaches with never a least
mishap. Skipper
trusts tiny Max at the controls,
as no one else* . . . And even as he speaks,
young Maxie surges
into a new high vantage, his whole torso thrust
upon the wheel to swerve left, thereby
to avert a drunk yachtman's
beeline charge

into our hull at midship . . . Suddenly Cap Rudolf
looms up tall behind him,
khaki-suited, all one faded beige hue
from collar to pants cuffs.
He seems triple
his son's height. Does he step near
to *spell* young Max, if the clash & frazzle
of sea traffic gets the upper
hand? *No way!* Cap floats
his open palm
over junior's bangs . . . He could retire
today, the Snapper's future
squared away in that paternal slouch of shoulder.

BONAIRE SEXTET

Bonaire Day, Flag Day. The whole island
　　shuts down—parades
　　　　and fetes to proclaim their independence.
　　　　　　Here the oldest citizens
　　　　are esteemed—not just patronized, as in the States—
we to be tutored or regaled by them in garden,

　　　　　　country road, marketplace;
　　and this morning, the musical seniors
　　　　　　shall play dance music for the holiday.
Our over-eighty band troop of six males assembles
　　　　　　toward the back
　　　　of the high grandstand in Helga's Park.
　　　　The tallest man poised
　　　　in the center, highlighted
　　　　by his prominent beak nose and Beanie Cap,
　　Derek performs
　　on his double-headed snare drums
　　loosely slung
　　round his neck by a thin leather strap.
　　　　The eldest gent
　　　　　　of the troop seeming but half

Derek's height, in his mid Nineties,
　　droops forward
　　　　a tad, just left of the center-pole man.
　　　　　　Aldo plays the Chac-Chac,
　　　shaking the blackish gourd with both hands, the beans
within slapped this way and that in odd counter-

　　　　point with the drumbeats,
　　the Chac-Chac stutterings pitched higher

and crisper. O wonderful it is to behold
how much Aldo is able to vary the rhythm and tone
of shaken beans
as he rotates the gourd, flat side
first turned one way,
then the other; next, he shifts
from up-down jerks to sideways moves followed
by intervals
of diagonal swings, and whichever
way he sweeps
the Chac-Chac his protrusive Adam's
Apple seems to do
a juggling act in his neck

that runs exactly counter to his dual-
handed shimmies
with the striped bean gourd. Farther left, Jake
gustily works open & closed
the tattered lung sacs of his old-world, silk-skinned
accordion: of a middle height, his high elbows

swerving in and out, he just
escapes clouting Aldo in the ear or jaw,
the latter short enough of stature to elude
those wicked elbow chops. Should Derek's drumsticks miss
the twin drums' taut
sheep-skin caps or slide off the rim,
they might catch Aldo
in the right eye or temple,
but the mishmash of aging reflexes undulate
in perfect sync,
the tottery ensemble wallowing
its way, atilt,
to a quirky sort of balance . . . Max

sweetly tootles
a clarinet at the snare drums'

far side, while two guitarists, at either end,
round out the troop,
all six tap-dancing, creakily, on the echo-
chamber of the grandstand's
plywood floor . . . syncopation of their thudding boot heels
rattling off a whole second wave of drum rolls.

THE ELECTRIFIER
(Maireau, The Grenadines)

Canoun to the North, Union
and Palm Island just Southeast—they're all
fully *electrified.* And Malcolm dreams of the first
electric power matrix for his home islet. Now he shows me
Maireau's future on the palm of my hand, no fortune teller who
traces lifelines of my prophecy, but light sorcerer mapping circuits,
drawing magnetic lines of force: power poles *here,* crisscrossing
power cables *there.* The wiring could revolve in concentric
circles, the lines of force swirling around hilltops
like my handprint whorls. As he illustrates
and explains the variants

of overhead or underground
wiring layout, he could be redesigning deep
patterns in my hand, perhaps juggling the vital check-
points and bloodlines of My Fate . . . So I pull my hand away
in alarm. *Not to worry,* he laughs. *In lieu of chalk blackboard,
we draft and plot on our hands.* That said, he clasps my red-ink pen
and scribbles wire graphs and crosshatching on his own virgin
palm. *Hey, those penmarks will stain like tattoos,* I say . . .
He's been to school for engineers. He knows the least
costly and most efficient ways to light up
his whole country's home-

scape. *Soon we'll put away
the hundreds of candles, scores of lanterns
and pocket flashlights—throw a single switch to illum-
inate Maireau's twin hillslopes like a pair of multicolored
Xmas trees* . . . He scrawls and strokes until his whole palm's one

crosshatched smear of red. As simple as that be his dream of lifting
his country from a Dark Age of gloom into starry constellations.
I who take electric-powered homes for granted can only gasp
at his eyes' fireup . . . Electronics seer, he visualizes
infrastructure of forever lit shacks. An over-
head bulb in every outhouse . . .

HARDHAT LIMBO

Seventeen men and boys in shiny yellow hardhats, bunched in the rear
stall of Dodge Pickup, bob over the bumps—their heads lolling
in sync like a jiggly bouquet of human dandelion blooms.
The driver floors the throttle in low gear: roars—
inchingly—up the steep grade. Halfway
to a hilltop, great swirls
of rain, little cyclones of gush, come
whipping down on the truck, and the laggard crew
howl in chorus, halting the transport car on the spot—
as if they'd whunked into a deer or calf, so sudden a braking
and tire burn of rubber. The workers cheer the foreman driver, who

starts to coast backwards down the hill. *No work today,* they shriek
with glee. *Hard rain's gonna fall, gonna fall,* they rasp & groan
in Bob Dylan guttural croaks. Rain puddles would loosen
their road tars & wall mortars, spoiling the seal.
Ah, they're all of one mind, so prone
to hot-tail it back home
for sweet holiday. The man at the wheel
coasts downhill and brakes in lunges, reversing
his gears, at last, as if waiting out the quick-switch
of weather. And no sooner does he speedup the backout, all rain
quits, cloud overcast cracks open like an axe-riven coconut, and Sun

pours forth its Golden Milk. Back into forward gear, zip-zip, cranks
the bossman to a fizzle of heartsick jeers from his men. Stolen
holiday! *Lost, O lost,* they bleat, a flock of betrayed
sheep. They scale hill steeps once more, leveling
out on the top of the rise, and worse
rain squall bears down—

to ecstatic hurrahs of the men, another
truckload of crew bringing up the rear . . . Both halt
and reverse. Rain whirligigs to shine. And a tug-of-war
between work and play resumes, yellow hardhats trapped in limbo,
hollers of joy fade to grunts: no play, no work. Six hour cul-de-sac. . . .

JAWBONERS

I lope
across the Interisland Ferry deck
and warily approach
a fracas at midship. Three women
in their Sixties perhaps—
all regular commuters—are loudly bickering
with the Collector of Tariffs. They dispute
the overblown cost
of transporting their wares. It's a routine
scuffle,
for one and all. Anyone can sense that
in sourness of the air
fluttering between them—bitter, acrid,
it's a dour scent peculiar
to their tone of vocalization. Yes, these money
tiffs seem endemic to a whole class of travel
folks. I'd bet on it!
They are playing out roles grown so familiar
to them,
they could sleep-jabber through the spat
and never slip up,
or miss a cue. He says, they mustn't under-
pay by five E.C. dollars . . .
Pshaw! He overcharges by ten, maybe even twenty,
E.C. dollars, say they . . . If they don't pay up
quick, he'll *impound*
their goods *posthaste*. He will *brook* no least
delays,
his patience wears thin, they'd better
not put his *resolves*
to the test, once he *Lays Down the Law*

for impudence—no way will he reverse his strict
verdict. *Put away those bribes,* he'll grimly say.
           I shan't be budged . . .
    Do they know he bluffs? And do his threats ring
            hollow?
                Perhaps. Brave souls, they do not quail
           or relent by a hair.
        Back and forth they haggle, their voices
          racing faster and faster—
    accents seem to thicken, and I'm losing the drift
of the words, so I tune out the chatter. I focus
        on their face moves.
    On both sides, the combatants rage to keep
            jawbones
             working in and out for a prescribed set
         number of yells. Throat
    or neck muscles, cut off from the usual
      brain-stem signals, may decide
    by their own volition when to quit. With no warning,
all four hasslers give out at once. No one recants,
        but their eyes bespeak
    verbal stalemate . . . And they're strangely happy!

SASSY BELLE

That older belle,
narrow-faced and hollow-cheeked, reclines, sprawled
across three of her bulky well-stuffed
duffelbags, each sack trailing
a knotted draw-cord. The fullest, which leaks
strings of beads & scarves at its maw, is crammed
with clothes & personal effects: this one she straddles
between her narrow thighs,
hugging it like a saddle; two others
bulging with foodstuffs,
bulbous squash, turnips, parsnips, and potato shapes . . .
She keeps eyeing six or seven more cartons
& bags heaped against the side rails,
wary of thieves or those over-fussy
customs louts. Given

a choice, she'd
sooner take her chances with the lowly pickpockets.
If the lawmen have it in for you, they rob
you three ways: impound your goods,
hit you with steep fines, and tack on a jail
sentence for good measure. Those sneak thieves
may steal you blind, or take only what they need to fend
off the cold or starvation
for one day—and that's an end to it.
But the Customs Devil
gets his *jollies* from nagging & scavenging helpless
tradeswomen, traveling sellers like herself.
Now in her Seventies, for *upwards*
of thirty years she's been hauling
her private cargoes

                              singlehandedly
          with never a partner or helpmate, and glad of it.
                Twice blessed, to be a shrewd trader
        and ever on her own . . . But I
                      find her grumpy & suspicious, always peeking
        back over her shoulder for a fancied enemy.
                      Hyper-alert. On the verge of mild hysteria throughout
                our trip. And not a few
        veteran deck blokes on shipboard
                              are prone to needle
                  and tease her. They love the verbal jousts, as does she,
        for all her braying and shrieks about harms
                              inflicted by her *abusers* . . . Perhaps
                one full hour before our arrival
                in Carriacou, she's

                              already begun
                  the laborious drudgery of hefting her scattered
                arsenal of baggage from the ship's hold
        to the main deck and exit gate.
                      She scoots down the spiral stairwells, then
        weaves back up the narrow steps puffily lugging
                      three boxes at once in net-bags strung over her shoulder,
                no idle boatswain lifting
        a finger to help her—even when
                              she gets trapped, frozen
                  halfway in a blockage of stair upsweep, unable to budge
        up or down for at least ten minutes, caught there
                              and cursing her luck, but never begging
                for help. Finally, she drops back down
                to the hold level

                              as she scrambles
                  for better access and footing, her load lightened.
                So many trips it takes her, I'm amazed

                                                                    129

at her strength—her arms brittle sticks,
> you can almost hear joints creak as she cranks
an overload . . . At last, when all crates are stacked
> for unloading, two dockhands poke fun at her knobby knees
> and scrawny bow-legged shanks.
She falls for it every time, getting
> riled to a vivid pitch
> of stomping her wood clogs on deck in time with tirade
> flow of cusswords—a pure unquenchable discharge.
> No way to stop her fluster motor until
> she burns up a few more gallons of mad-
> lady voice fuel. . . .

FOUR SISTERS

Under fair sky,
taking my first hours-long brisk hike
from Carriacou's remote south beach northeast
back to Hillsborough, I set out just before sunset and clamber
past twilight into deep dusk
in so few minutes, it seems, and wouldn't you know, my flashlight
goes dead just as the road narrows.
Fear not, my friends had mocked. *If you but follow*
the main drag, you can't
get lost. But in tar-black dark, who can tell weed-riddled
patchup of road
from side paths
that fork off, at intervals. So I find myself coming upon
abrupt dead end,
and know myself for lost . . . Peering through woods-
brake, I can make out dim auto
headlamps in the distance. I cut through the little patch of forest
and make a dash to head off
the vehicle. The mercifully slow driver, so stunned to see
a lost foreign pale-skinned gent   bareheaded
in rolled-up trousers   come rocketing
from roadside brush

like startled quail
into his bearing-down-hard trajectory,
brakes to a snappy halt. The front sidedoor
flies open to offer me a lift before I can think to thumb-beg
for it, all welcome blurted
in the gravelly rasp of aged voice *(O if ever turn of tongue*
incarnated pure pulse of helper's
hand, the magic of utterance now felt so) . . . Soon
installed beside one

very thickly bifocal-laden man bowed over the wheel,
those heavy specs
drooped so low
on his nostrils, a small miracle of balance keeps them
from sliding off
to the floor of the Fifties-style VW beetle.
Father Mulligan and Father
Sheehan, both Irish, are co-priests of the Roman Catholic Church, here.
What with Sheehan off-isles
this month, my new helpmate Mulligan divides his squeezed time,
about equally, between church duties
and building, he alone sole architect
and contractor

for all church
construction or restorative labors
in Carriacou and neighbor-isle Grenada,
but never too busy to rescue a lost lamb just strayed away
from the flock. *Yours truly,*
do you mean? No verbal reply, but he squints a yes-nod. Peeps,
at last, from two tiny women
hunkered down small in backseats, so noiseless
before now, I wonder
if they held their breaths. *Are you two with the Church?*
obtusely I ask,
two nuns, both
out of Habit, garbed in drab loose ash-colored smocks
and beige pullover
sweaters. More nods, in tandem. *And which Faith*
do you espouse?. . . O Roman
Catholic, this nation's passion and High Calling. Ours, as well . . .
Do you know Mother Theresa,
young fellow? Mulligan interjects. For all answer, my jaw
drops open. *These two are HER children,*

he exults. *O my, you're her DAUGHTERS,*
I sigh (holding

down a fluttery
gasp). *Indeed not, we're SISTERS!,*
voices rising to a brittle staccato now.
They arrived here just last month, *Four Sisters* ferried out
together by cheap freight-
barge carrying huge cargoes of rice and beans direct from India
(that numberless bevy of sisters,
too, *a crop* of sorts), the other pair of Church
Ladies from their elite
small quorum now resting in the church annex that Father
Mulligan himself
built last summer
for their troop's harborage. *Where is your home?* I ask,
still not letting it
sink in. *O here, wherever a challenge to our Faith
and Mission is strongest. We set
sail from our City of Birthright, Calcutta, some six weeks ago.*
As it happens, these women
had never before left their native Asian terrain, and given
the likely scope of island-nurturing project
they've just begun, they may never go
back to Calcutta . . .

*Father, don't miss
your turn,* murmurs the near loquacious
Sister Esmeralda, tapping his shoulder
to signal the precise instant for him to take a sharp left
at the narrow side-road
forking through a tall archway to the churchyard. *The entry gate
is just here,* she softly chirps.
More shoulder nudgings. He seems to look beyond
the gate, or above it,

as if it's a blank void—but follows her lead, even so.
I hear a faint
rustle & scrape,
whilst he grazes front fender on the brass gatepost.
The two Nun zealots
exchange wary glances. I can see they've muddled
through such minor collisions
before, though I sense Esmeralda's struggle to ward off an impulse
to seize the wheel from him . . .
Parting words, we four now standing in a circle beneath
the bright streetlamp: Father Mulligan
turns my book over and over, squinting
hard to descry

tallish letters
of my title. Those milky-white lenses
magnify the print just enough. *Ah, GOD'S
MEASUREMENTS,* he rattles off, fondly inviting me to Sunday
High Mass in the next breath.
Now the women are thumbing pages, asking a few routine questions
about my year in Japan—the size
and beauty of the giant Buddhas . . . When they first
have some leisure time,
they hope to read my poems, which cue prompts me to ask,
shyly, *How long do*
you mean to stay
in Carriacou? Forever! Dipa beams back, without pause.
We shall never leave
this place. Always there will be four of us here.
The whole flock—perhaps two dozen
Women of the Cloth—will be shuffled about, rotated from isle
to isle of the Grenadines
and beyond, like a portable lending library of Lady Clerics!
Always, others of the Faith will take our place.
In Fours. No matter which, we're all the same
One. Four in One.

GRENADA BIRTHDAY SONG

One day jet
split between two island
nations, St. Vincent and Grenada—
it's the Eve of my birthday. *Fifty nine. Split.*
Starry night. Sipping a beer on the rooftop lounge, I
await the local chums for dinner. Three tables
down, an aging gent, Telly Savalas near-
clone, drinks toast to young
slender blonde:

two champagne glasses
meet with surefire honeymooner's
click; while I, trying to not eavesdrop
or peep, catch snippets
of her thick Slav accent
meshing with his refined Bostoner's
elocution. I keep
turning away, but he glimpses the volume
of poetry I scan, my swift cursory meanderings
across the page,
distracted, as I wait to get on
with the magical sky's

High Fever,
O who can explain, it's
one of those rarely certain times,
a blessedness in the air. . . . Ben elongates
himself to six two or three, saunters to my table
and asks after the Robert Lowell *Dolphin*
I've been skimming (fellow Bostonian,
no less, so he presumes
certain rights;

or may it be his love
of poetry that propels him
my way?)—he gets on my case, waylays me
for cad interloper
on post-Wedding Day gala
best cheer. But when he discerns
I'm a poet, myself,
in exile for my Birthday Eve, to boot,
he explodes with ardor, reciting—without preface
or apology—
fifteen strophes of *his* long poem,
songlike, composed

thirty years
before, paean of praise,
celebrating Israel's survivorship
of Jews in World history! From time to time,
his voice breaks into orthodox church-opera vibratos
of a Cantor hymning the Yom Kippur liturgy.
And don't you know, he walked away
from promising career
as a Rabbi

in midtown Boston
synagogue to work in Labor
Relations in D.C., that lucrative post
which he vacated—early
retirement—just last week,
to wed his third bride in Daytona
Beach, Fla. *What's next?*
They'll settle in Miami when they wind up
this two-week stint in Grenada. Eloise, 20-year-old
Yugoslav
immigrant, who, after 3 years'
work as a domestic

on short-term
Alien Visa, had just filed
her papers for naturalized American
Citizenship, when she collided with our Ben
Golden in civil court parlor annex, fell and bruised
her shin on antique brass-studded lounge chair.
He'd caught her wrist (small comfort),
steered her to a first aid
station, melted

in *Love's Labours Lost*
with svelte Eloise on the spot.
Just launched from the heavyweight swash-
buckler realm of D.C.
business and industry, what
a Godsend for him to be swept back,
tonight, into his twin
lost worlds. Poetry & orthodox Judaism!
He'd never lost his perfect pitch of Cantor's warbly
operatics
after three decades of virtual
abstinence, disavowal

of all churchly
gifts. Our hearty embrace,
Ben Golden and I, or so we avouch,
can be no mere happy coincidence, both expat
American Jews splicing tag ends of Wedding to Birthday
fetes; our meeting was charmed by that starry
blaze, a beneficent hex—two poets
hung up on God, song spiel
& Israel's Fate.

V.

STEPS OF THE SNAKE

Eiffel, Eiffel (after the great tower of Paris),
O Eiffel Francis . . .
One hundred seven years next week,
but who'll remember her birthday? She's outlived
all her friends, all
six sons: the fifth, Louis, was famed Carib Chief
for some fifteen years, then died—
twenty years back—
in his Seventies . . . She has social *bent,* strong wit,
quick bite & snap
in a contest of repartee, which
I discern in her swift banter of greetings to us,
her warm exchanges

with Victor. But alas, few visitors, ever fewer,
patronize her hut,
whether friends or foreigners.
Son Louis was the last in a long line of chiefs
who spoke—ably,
if not fluently—the old Carib tongue, she herself
knowing only a few sparse words,
native Creole French
her one dialect for daily commerce. So starved
she is for company!
Do folks forget she still holds court,
and holds up her end of tête-à-tête far better
than most; tireless,

she outlasts those half her age (or halved again),
all staying power . . .
Her narrow teetery shack, upright
but atilt, seems a cross between a phonebooth
and an outhouse

in shape, and not much larger. Skewed at the bottom
of a long steep decline in the swale,
     her place shuts out
        the frail or lame, inaccessible to anyone but
     the most sure-footed.
No true path leads here. False starts
        end in deep pits like half-dug wells; or boulders,
remnants perhaps

        of a recent rock-slide . . . Vic drops off loose sandals,
     takes one barefooted
leap to the floor level of Eiffel's
        cozy hut propped on stilts, and answers her voice
           of welcome belted,
        hoarsely, out. I'm bent over now, unlacing my shoes—
but Victor lifts my arm, saying *No need,*
     no need to soil feet,
        do keep your footwear. I scramble about the interior
     few floor inches,
each foot a cumbersome unwieldy
        hulk, my shoes as overblown in this snug enclosure
as two newly dugup

        and exposed tree stumps; the unsightly heels could be
     raw seeping root ends,
soil clumps spilling from my insoles:
        corkscrews or spirochetes . . . *Not to worry, stay put*—
        they both implore.
     Eiffel shrinks in a recess, her arms two crossed kite
sticks folded over her scrub-board chest,
     her one drab garment
        a narrow tubular sack: knobs poking out, here & there,
     could be loose turnips
or rutabagas, her moves all swervy
        joint wobbles . . . I straddle the one narrow cracked bench,
while Vic and Eiffel

squat in opposite corners. Now taking a giddy pride
in this boxy house
her husband left her, some five decades—
her four frailest sons' lifetimes—ago, she invites me
to scan her treasures,
eight family photographs thumbtacked to the wall
behind her back. And we three strike up
a trialogue: Vic fields
my questions, gyrating between my Anglo and Eiffel's
Creole French dialect.
As in subtitles for foreign films,
the German actors talking fast, long monologues condensed
into tiny captions,

you know you're missing big chunks of talk, so now. . . .
Her house near the sea,
her dead husband was a master fisherman,
one son for fifteen years the Carib Chief. Both heroes.
Their lives milestones
and legends to their heirs. Her son the last Chief to speak
the defunct tongue . . . She springs erect, waves
her arm in the doorway
slot, and highlights the cliff ridge overhanging the shore.
That bluff arcs down
seaward in one long graceful curve
like a sand dune's sweep, rises once in a serpentining loop,
then drops: *Escalier*

Tetchein, it's called. *Steps of the Snake.* A huge snake,
thick as a dinosaur's
neck and twice as long, crawled up
this cliff. It rose from the sea, leaving its wriggly
furrowing prints
at every level as it slithered to the peak, then hid
in a cliff-top cavern. That snake
was the source and keeper

of all tobacco crops. Those seeking fresh tobacco plugs
for pipes must plead
with the snake in old Carib lingo,
sung in rhyme with a true old-time accent. Chief Louis
sang his chapter

and verse of prayer for twelve successive twilights
at the dark cave mouth.
On the thirteenth eve, as he intoned
those sacred words, the snake thrust its great wide jaws
through the cave gullet,
spat brown trickles through its fangs, and vomited up
a rich harvest of tobacco leaves,
tobacco seeds spewn
as well, for later plantings. Louis, first and last chief
to unlock the snake's
secret of good smokes, was most loved
for his tobacco chants. To this day, tribal smokers praise
his gift . . . Now Madame

Eiffel bids me to stroll down to the seashore inlet
nearest her doorstoop
and call out to the lost Carib Souls
trapped below the tide-rumpled strand. If I can utter
my summons in true dirge
wail, the roof of their prison grotto will rise a notch
and they will creep out, one by one,
to serenade me
with sad tales of their eternal lockup. *But beware,*
she says. *If you step*
too close, the trapdoors may swing open
and you'll be sucked down under, quick as a snake-tongue
flicks the passing gnat.

THE SACREDNESS OF FINGERS

I.

Eiffel Francis, the oldest Carib Matriarch, berates
the modern custom of burying our newly deceased at four P.M. sharp
   no matter what time they died—whether the selfsame day
or the day before. Four O'clock,

                    at the earliest,
   is blindly affixed for burials. *When will they learn?* she says.
                Either they bury
     folks too early or too late; but there are *best times,*
       worst times, to plow them under. In her youth,
the custom—rarely broken—was to wait twenty-four hours from dying
             to gravedig, *never*
       less. Indeed, many calamities have sprung
        from wrongly-timed

   burials. O she could cite dire cases and proofs
aplenty, but one close to her heart must suffice . . . Cousin Hazel,
   a widow of means, childless, was afflicted with double
pneumonia which—if coupled

               with her *Rheumatic*
Heart—spelled certain demise. Haplessly, her doctors broke
          the news to Hazel
   and her nearest kin: her hours were numbered, no way
      could she outlast the coming twilight, dusk,
this prognosis uttered at noon Tuesday. Did she have any death-bed
          last wish, they asked.
      Only that her precious jewels, the main bulk
        of her much-vaunted

wealth, be buried with her in the plush casket.
They were sacred to her, amongst them holy relics she'd collected
    at ancient shrines, and they might serve her Spirit
in the Life to Come. Heirless,

                    she chose to abscond
    with her valuables into the grave; whereupon her elder brother
                    raised a great fuss
    at the death-watch vigil, pleading with her to divide
        her bounty with her two nieces and nephew
up to her last dying expulsion of breath. But she remained adamant
                    in her fierce resolve.
        Not one pearl, nor ruby or emerald locket
            would she relinquish . . .

    2.

    "In those days they could hardly wait to put away
the Dead, they'd rush, rush to dispatch the corpse beneath the sod,
    be the victim pauper or well-to-do . . . Less than two hours
after death, the last sprinkles

                    of soil are patted
    flat over Hazel's tomb. And just four hours later brother Ralph,
                masked and camouflaged
        in skin-tight diver's black wetsuit, comes scrambling
            on all fours into the graveyard lugging shovel,
tire-iron for prying, and a wrench or two. In no time at all, the Tomb
                Door is exposed, yanked
            open, all bolts unscrewed. Most of those gem-
                stones, bejeweled rings,

    brooches & pendants are bestrewn, helter-skelter,
about the coffin interior's velour linings; but a few luminescent

bracelets and necklaces adorn the body of the cadaver,
many pins clasped to her dress

and diamond tiaras
affixed to her high-piled pompadour, all as was designated
by the instruction kit
she left for the embalmer and undertaker. Now Ralph
gives himself over to a frenzy of grasping
the loot, snapping up random loose stones and attached jewels, alike,
with indiscriminate
haste—yanking bracelets from wrist, necklace
from her comely neck,

then tearing out handfuls of hair from her scalp
along with coronets and knotted fasteners. All the while, he keeps
revving himself up with chants and fatuous wild slogans
of self-boosting. *Such foolish*

waste. What possible
use can she have for this opulent display? Our poor children
need clothes, revenue
for school tuition hikes. At last, wife Beulah and I
can pay for travels abroad, never before
within reach. Now what harm can come from robbing the dead? Ourselves,
Hazel's true family,
deprived and betrayed by her crazy death-bed
whims! . . . Ralph's plunder

proceeds without hitch, or pause to reflect,
until he notes that Hazel's small hands are curled into tight fists
as if they are clutching something. Ah, he must possess
this last treasure she prizes

so highly, her hands
would keep their secret palm-pressed for eternity. As he tries

to unclench the fingers
and break her grip, he catches a whiff of living palm
sweat, then sees fresh droplets blister upon
her forehead, and before he can register his shock enough to cry out
in terror, her lips
have begun to form whispered words that rise
to murmurs and, at last,

to full-throated voice. *O my brother, you may take*
whatever accursed jewels you wish from the casket, and I forgive it—
but please, O please, take care not to break my fingers . . .
And in truth, when he started

to fiercely unlock
and manipulate those frozen fingers she swiftly came back, came
from wherever it is we go when we go off to that place
between worlds—that narrow isthmus between
life and death, where some souls may tarry and hover or stay suspended
in an undetected
not-quite-visible half-life. There you wait
for the ghostly signal:

whichever one is stronger, the Grand Prompter
nudging you this way and that, prodding you to take a last dreamy
tilt forward over the finish line, end zone into Death;
or jogging you into a topple,

sliding backwards
perhaps, luckily, into the leftover life not quite squelched—
a moist vacuum cup
still waiting to suck you into its concave hollow
if only you lean just so delicately, ease-
fully, slowly, back into its toehold . . . And yes, for all her talk
about keeping finger

digits intact and undislodged, it's the tip
of her left small toe

she finds—as she wriggles it—that commences
the wobbles that teeter her back . . . First sign, palm sweat. Then,
her lips move. Whispers rise to full voice. Eyes open.
But he sees only blank whites

staring noplace;
he yells and runs as she pops, bolt upright, in the casket—
& never looks back.
They find him raving in mid-river, who now mutters
about Hell's Demons sent out to punish him:
he keeps immersing his head, inept tries to drown himself, drown out
all sight of the living
dead sister he robbed. Pleads to undo the sin,
but his mind has snapped,

and crackbrained he stays. Unhinged. Meanwhile,
Hazel wanders from the grave to his house, meets sis-in-law Beulah
at the door, who faints dead away on the spot. Her son
can't rouse her for days, feverish

moanings and outbursts
in her deep sleep. But Hazel lives for many years in robust good
health, confounding doctors
& pallbearers, as well, who'd transported her seeming-dead
carcass to the gravesite in that open coffin;
they know they saw her unbreathing frame in their hands . . . It was she,
Hazel, who traveled
to foreign lands on the proceeds and income
from gems sold at auction."

BOILING LAKE

(The Carib Reserve, Dominica, 1937)

"Many years before
        they built the first road between Roseau—the Capital
    City—and Salybia,
  women had to hike to town on monthly
        shopping missions. Three or more gals would team up
            for safety and comradeship;
        at best, it took them three whole days to walk each way.
They carried only a little money,
      some fruit and eggs,
          maybe nuts. About halfway to Roseau, they were relieved
  to come upon Boiling Lake.
They supposed they knew which months, each year,
        the lake was moderately hot—and those were the times
the newcomers liked best.

            Youthful women
        might wish to take a quick dip, popping in & out
          and perhaps scrubbing a few bundles
    of laundry. But the elder ladies
           always warned the reckless young niece
or friend. *Stay out. Don't risk your tender legs
          to be burned and permanently scarred. Who can be sure
      when the few safest days*
occur, cool enough for dunking
            or swimming? The bold lass
      might be testing the surface with her fingertips
or toes first, then hold them up to us, saying—
           See, no harm in it. Where's the heat,
  where the boilup you fear so much?
      But that mere toe-

dipping's no proof
        of the secret depths. Magic spirits down below, hell-
    bent to fool us, may trick
anyone into scalding her heels and shins;
        or worse pain, if we dunk quick our private parts.
            Shrewd demon may hide down under—
        cunning he be, so fast to switch from chills to fevers,
joking water games to tease and test us.
    But he won't play
        safe—the sudden boilups can kill! Best times, we can see
        thick cushion of steam & mist
hovering, cloudlike, over the surface. Then,
        we know the lake is up to full boil, and we can cook
our carryall viands.

            We tie up eggs
        in our handkerchief and dangle them from a pole—
            a fishing rod is best, or bamboo switch
        that keeps limber for good swing,
            good snap. Now we're dipping those eggs
in the lake for three or four minutes, so fast,
            they boil hard and firm up. And we mustn't lose count,
        whatever number we cook, large
or small—it could be just three eggs,
            but maybe ten or twelve—
        we always add one extra, one more than we plan
to eat, since we know that one shall be missing
                when we come to pull up our kerchief.
    No matter how tight we tie the knots,
        and no matter

how strong & unfrayed
        the cloth, one egg will vanish. The Spirit of the Lake
    snaps it up—it's a payment,
or good-will offering. Oh, there could be

most any number to start with, forty beans, nine yams,
      six potatoes, a dozen figs,
    just one is always spirited away . . . We can never be sure
when it will be snatched, often at the start—
    for if we check
      our cooking in the first few seconds, it may truly be gone.
    (The linen never rips or tears,
so how did it get out?) . . . I still remember,
      bananas were my favorite snack food on the long hikes.
They cook so fast,

          you dip them
      and flip them out, already they're done. Slide off
        peel & eat. Once we had just two, the lake
took one banana, we had to divvy up
        the other. If we had only one fruit,
forget it. Eat it raw. The lake can't know
        you don't share what stays uncooked. But if you partake
    of those bubbling waters,
they you must pay" . . . .
          Once in midsummer,
      Eiffel and four lady friends
started off on the usual pilgrimage to Roseau
for shopping. As they passed the Boiling Lake,
        young Alicia—still in her teens—grew
tired and short of breath. She couldn't
    go on. The others

were too quick, the pace
      on trail was *too snappy a clip,* she said: it made her
dizzy, all stomach-whoozy,
so they should carry on without her. She'd
      rest up by lakeside and await their return, days
      hence . . . True, needs abounded
    at home, too many children went hungry, had no clothes

to wear, or suffered ills for lack of medicine.
    No time to lose,
        they must leave her behind; but she promised to stay near
    lake's edge for days, or until
they'd buzz back, laden with supplies. And off
        they went . . . The first day, she took her rest, idled
& dozed on the shores—

            nor strayed afar.
      She dared not even dangle her fingers or toes
        in the offshore shallows, the steam-
clouds fair warning of the sizzly
            currents below. The second day, she grew
restless & bored, wandering to the woodside
        to pick wildflowers, but she was distracted by fallen
    tool or some implement
aglitter in tall grass of the thicket.
      She bent over and plucked
    the dazzling slender wand—ah, it was a golden
comb. She ran its teeth through her dun hair
        a few times, and the heat it gave off
thrilled her scalp. She sang her love,
    and sensed her dark

brown hair brightening,
      gradually, to the comb's sunflowery gold. *Could this be*
the color of dreams? She tucked
that comb in the braid behind her left ear,
      and started up the path toward a cottage that looked
      inviting, but vacant perhaps.
    Halfway there, the path swerved and reversed—she heard
a swish of wings aflutter in her ears
    and found herself
    circling back to the lakeside spot where she'd just begun
her stroll. She felt she must visit

this ivy-covered quaint shanty, so she sprinted
            toward its doorway as fast as she could run down the path
thinking to overtake

                    the odd reverse
            effect by sheer speed and hard looking sideways
                after her course. But alas, there was
        no outsmarting the trick path,
                    which always pirouetted her right back
    to where she began. Of course, she couldn't tell
                when the magical transport occurred; it seemed to take
            less time than a sneeze, say.
She held her breath, and tried not to blink
                her eyes, so as to maintain
        her focus unshakably; but some little whirlwind
    seemed to lift her spinning back to the point
                    of onset. Now she tried to be clever
        and mischievous, in hopes to befuddle
            the playful imp

of the path. She walked
            in zigzags, or even backwards—she'd get just so close
        to the colorful dwelling,
    no closer, and back she was swept, her hair
            streaming out behind her as if she were carried off
                by a horse or a witch's
            broom. After six failed tries to reach the hut, she plucked
    the gilded comb from her hair-bob & flung it
        hard into the grassy
            copse where she first spotted its glow, saying *I give you*
        back your gold-toothed comb, O Spirit
    of the Boiling Lake. Please forgive my bold theft,
            my greedy ways . . . Now she found she could stroll, undetoured,
to the hut's gateway,

and she skipped,
joyously, up the porch steps. The front door stood
ajar, she pushed it and sidled within.
A few cassavas were hanging
from the lintel, and she freely partook
of their ripe fruit. Alicia gulped the morsels
down ravenously, as if she were starving. She chomped
and spat, untidily,
thinking she was alone; but a portly seaman
entered the house, hoisting
a long stringer of fish, and he started to howl
in terror. He mistook her for a demon,
since she was slavering so boorishly
while she gobbled cassavas—he begged her
not to eat him.

Truly, this man feared
for his life and tried to appease her with flapping fish
extended toward her drool-streaked
jaws; but she laughed & stroked his hand with kind
caress, saying *I'm just a poor human like yourself, no
monster. I need a shelter
for the night, may I stay in your homestead?* Then he kissed
her hand and cried tears of welcome, so happy
to care for *a pregnant
mother-to-be.* A great shock to her it was, how'd he guess
she was with child when she, herself,
hadn't a clue! Well, he knew what he knew, she mustn't
doubt him . . . And that night, the Kalbasplon bird kept crying
overhead, *caw-caw-caw*

as it swooped
thither & yon: *proof positive,* he said, that she'd
soon bear a son. She agreed to accept
his offer; her new friend would nurse

and protect her. . . . Days later, when Eiffel
and the ladies returned to Boiling Lake, puffing
under a load of viands secured from the open market
in Roseau, their young friend
Alicia had vanished. They paced back
& forth along the shores
of Boiling Lake calling her name, softly at first,
as if whispers might bring her back sooner;
then scolding at the top of their voices—
impugning her not to worry them so,
she'd scared them

half to death. They guessed
she perhaps had fallen into the lake, or was drawn—
by foolish whim or impulse—
to bathe in its alluring waters, then was boiled
and shriveled to death before she could climb back out
like an egg or spiny lobster
simmered in its shell. (But none dared utter such a dread!)
Or at best, she may have regained her strength
and trotted back home,
alone, before the first nightfall. But as they soon learned,
poor Alicia failed to make her way
back to the Carib Reserve. O lost . . . Months later,
they visited an augurer who, for a modest fee, employed
magnets and charms to plumb

dark whereabouts
of Lost Souls. Quickly she gleaned that the wayward
Alicia was neither lost nor scalded
to death in those super-hot
waters of the lake, as they feared. Instead,
she was the thriving mother of a newborn baby
boy—two weeks old, and tended by a kindly fisherman
who lived in the cottage

hidden in wooded retreat behind the lake.
              But his house had fallen
          under the spell of a sorceress. While their friend
     and child were safe, the pair had crossed over,
                unwittingly, into the slant Other World
      realm of bodiless spirits: whose fleshly
         shapes remained—

for a limited time—
       intact and whole in the cottage. But to win them back,
    the friends would have to perform
magic rites in the near environs of the fisher-
       folk's shanty, *and soon,* if they hoped to break the spell
         before Alicia and her babe
      were too far gone. She bid them make haste to Boiling Lake,
to travel at night and be vigilant to arrive
    in good time to prepare
       enchantments that would undo the odd witchery before daybreak.
    They put great store by the prudent words
of their hired conjuror, and followed her wise counsel
      to the letter. Eiffel Francis, our amazing talespinner, took
charge of the rescue

              mission, herself
       seven years into her eleventh decade today.
         Four ladies of the original troop,
     led by Eiffel, transported
           a good supply of candles and matches
to light up winding paths to the lake. Luckily,
        it was a brilliant fullmoony night, and they picked
      their sinuous way swiftly—
without mishap—to the appointed dwelling.
        As coached, they'd collected
     vials of their own spittle and would now distribute
   small droplets, at regular intervals, to earth

plots surrounding the house—calling out
Alicia's name as they circled the grounds.
No one answered

their calls. But when Alicia's
baby cried withindoors, all the tiny sprinkles of spit
replied: they echoed his howls
with little squeaks and mewlings, as foretold
by their spiritual helpmate. It was a true miracle
to hear all those wee voices
warbling like an omnipresent choir of sad babies linked
in a chain around the whole circumference
of the house. The women now
waited in patience for a further response. That noisy chorus
of counter-cries grew louder
and higher in pitch, when suddenly Alicia sprang
from the door—her son in arms—thrilled at sight of four
friends poised for her return.

DIVING INTO THE STONE

1. Flight from the Mother Stone

This morning, we drive
beyond all posted roads or trodden pathways across blank desert
to the remote sacred sites—each rock, cave or mesa
a locus of magic energies: myths were hatched here, great legends
surviving hundreds of years

still yoked
to geologic formations that fed the dreams
of early wayfarers and the native
Arawaks alike . . . That T-shaped tower,
a prodigy of nature, casts its shadow
on the three rocks one hundred meters beyond,
and downhill: it affords the exact time of day
at any moment, from dawn
to dusk. Perfect unwavering
clock! A ready-made
geologic timepiece, for anyone who's blessed
with the gift to read the land's message.
Forget hourglass. Water clock.
Solar Clock, this last, a reading
of rock & shadows,

light sliding across rock
at rising and falling angles—perhaps the best way to tell time
is to measure the tilt of sun across stone, gauging
lengths of shadow . . . Many years back, the Simacan, aged holy man
& augurer, took up residence

at the foot
of this colossal T of limestone. He'd sleep
on a flat rock bed, round-edged rock
for pillow. He chanted the future
to passersby. His predictive powers,
though limited, proved to be all-but-flawless
within the bounds of his supposed parameters . . .
I walk up the ledge steps
to a cliff shelf of that great T,
would-be time-reader, I;
then pondering three spaced out rocks below,
I summon the holy Simacan who lived here
all-year-round & told which times
were best to travel, to hunt boars,
to catch rare schools

of fish. Best times, always,
there be to plant crops, to conceive child—best names to choose
for children. He foretold when rains will come, which
stars to follow for safe travels, which stars to find the way home
when lost. All these riddles

solved, enigmas
unraveled, by the resident shaman: *hanging*
out, in love with tales told by a play
of light and shadow, shadow and light,
on those three desert rocks . . . One day
before, an artist's painting gave me the rooted
man-tall figure of the Simacan, long silver hair
outspread richly on his back
& shoulders, holding an oaken staff
unstooped, unstooped! No cane,
no prop to his nonagenarian stance; but rather,
a tool for taking the stars' quick measure
or sighting any lay of the land

under the slant light. And which, then,
        may be the truest

    portrayal of this desert
scene? The painter's blaze of color, or my teetering half-balanced
    view from rock ledge today? Perhaps neither. I find
I need both, equally . . . On to the Bonaire stone we go. Few visitors,
        before me, has Minister-of-

        Culture Franz
    escorted to this heart stone, soul stone, mystic
        King Rock of the land. And it *is* heart-
    shaped, I think. Lordly massive hunk
            of volcanic rock, sculptural and glowy-
    black—Rodin's thinker comes to mind. This boulder,
            the only bulk visible anyplace in our wide stretch
        of desert waste, island of black
rock in a sea of yellow-white sand . . .
            Take your time. Oh, write
        your notes in your timeless journal, says Franz,
    who now abandons me. And off he goes
            into wide-open plain for an hour—
    to weep and pray, tears and prayer
        his diurnal habit

    and ritual . . . I'm searching
for the way in, the way in—sole entryway to this undoubted one
of the many worldwide myths of rebirth. I, an utter
outsider . . . (*What are* my *rights?* I'd asked. *As good as anyone's,*
        yours. Or perhaps better

        than most, allowed
    Franz. *You, who have bravely gulped the waters*
        & winds of so many Carib isles, so alive
    to the best life of this region. No one,

it may be, is more eligible for a rebirth
through the Bonaire Stone. But one condition of entry—
for my rites of passage—I fail of: yes, despite all
my desultory wanderings alone,
my veerings to one coast or the other
throughout Bonaire, exploring
outer fringes and pockets of the interior, as well,
I have not yet shambled into my wild donkey
nor heard his harsh and strident brays.
How, then, can I know if I arrive
at true gateway

into a next life of Being
until my donkey shrieks? *When you have Right Faith, and not before,*
the mad creature will burst from the bush & take you
into its trance of rapture—then you shall clamber up to the Birth
Stone & stand on the verge.

Don't give up
the search. Your rough brute *awaits you.*) As Franz
departs, I'm a prickly mix of shivers
and hots, caution and daring. I find
my legs climbing the knobby sides of whale-
bulk of rock, my hands slithering into slots
& dents my eyes cannot make out before I think to try.
You cannot scale the steep
wavy sides, so acute is the grade
of slope, my brain warns—
but my hands & feet take charge: they act with a will
of their own, more like paws or talons than human
extremities. I watch them leading me
from ridge to the next bulbous stone
knuckle. I'm helpless

to forestall that pitch
and thrust of my limbs, it will take command of me with its mindless
steady progress. Perhaps I black out halfway to the roof,
since I snap to attention as I catch myself peering down a chimney-
like burrow in the boulder's

peak. I unfold,
creakily, to my full height on a topmost bulge
(I could be Ahab propped on the White
Whale's skull bumps), and fight off
impulse to dive into the gorge. My mind
comes back, Will returning to my arms & legs
as I edge back down the slippery black glacier. *Be
emptied,* I tell my fingers.
*Go back, back to the natural rhythm
of pure flowingness. Be
mindful in care, but* unminded *for dreamy free-flow
moves as you drift back to terra firma* . . . And when
I touch down upon sandy cracked floor,
eroded from months of drought, no earth
has ever seemed more

the mother to my aches
and twinges. I fall to my face and grapple the sandy waste—grind
my chin & knees & shoulders, one by one, into cradling
grit of fine-ground pebbles and gravel . . . Franz finds me dusty gray,
ash-colored from scalp to

socks. Every patch,
all exposed inches of my skin and garb, reduced
to a single dust-bin nocolor. Now he pats
sooty flecks of volcanic slag from my hair,
slapping little dust clouds from my shirt
and cutoff shorts. He laughs outright when I admit
I clambered my way to the great skylight in the roof

but quailed with fear, helpless
to bring myself to slide down the tunnel
into the hidden maze. What if
I could never find my way out of its dark labyrinth?
I hate my cowardice, and cringe at a chance missed . . .
It's too soon, he says. *You're not ready*
to cross over—pray give yourself
more time. Take heart.

2. *Wild Donkey*

Franz, my deliverer, bends
from the waist
and urges me to follow his lead. We each take up
two handfuls of warm sand. *Now*
press your hands
together, he says, *letting the excess sand sift*
between your fingers & hold
this pose, lightly,
as in prayer. Identity always
is conflict, two
sides of your being at odds, at war with each other.
The power-hungry Fire Snake
within your breast
may be calmed by the Dove of Gentleness. Now the dual
fighting parts of you, at last,
are at peace. Safe.
You become your undivided
Being, in touch
with your feelings, at one with the Planet . . .
I step

on a fallen limb of cactus
and squeal, a few

long spines piercing my rubber shoe sole, and Franz
          snaps up the offensive branch.
     Next, he pokes it
          into his arm, repeatedly.
     Swellings, hivelike,
appear in two rows down his forearm. But he smiles,
          saying—*We are too shut off*
from pain. I am
a part of Nature. I must partake of hurt, of wounding,
          to be steeped in life that reeks
all about us. Hence
          I entrust my skin to fullest
brunt . . .
               Minutes
later, a wild donkey crosses our path. O too hungry
          for comfort, so many ribs
     showing, I think.
And I shy away. Without pause, Franz puts his fingers
          under the donkey's snout
     and murmurs, chummily,
          you must risk the creature's
     bite, even prompt
the animal to nibble you, smoochy little love bites,
          to come into his ambiance—
     slowly, real trust
will build. It's best not to be too safe if you wish
          to be in touch, in touch.
     That said, he boldly
          thrusts his whole bare palm
     in donkey's drool-
slimed mouth, caressing its throat with his free hand. . . .

3. *Earth Kissed*

I mustn't lose heart,
Franz comforts me. Many others from foreign lands, like myself,
despite failed tries
to squirm and slither through the magic tunnels, grooves,
and passageways of the birth stone, have solved
the riddle of the maze—and embraced, finally, their *second* bursting
alive . . . Just this week,
while acting as tour guide for Alice, Dutch
lady Head of Unesco

from Amsterdam, and Mortimer,
a lawyer from British Columbia, Franz beheld
surprise drama of metamorphosis. Less than an hour
it took . . . After three previous visits, seven fumbled attempts
to negotiate passage through the Bonaire stone
and hatch a new birth, Mortimer hadn't lost good faith. The Spirit,
borne of his many cave hikes,
prevailed. Often losing himself in enchanted
grottoes for hours at a time, once
for a whole day,
equipped only with canteen,
a walking staff and a vague map that Franz
had dashed off to give him an idea of possible escape routes
if he should lose his way in the labyrinth
of crisscrossing loops and caverns—Mortimer found he had *quaffed
deeply of the wonders*
of this eight-tiered land of coral shelf layered
upon shelf, each level

honeycombed, socketed
with its own independent hookup of juxtaposed caves and crypts:
a topography, say,
of swiss cheese blown up, inflated, into a land mass. . . .

I'll give it one last try, Mort keeps saying,
huddled in the Nissan Pathfinder's back seat and staring upon brilliant
midday desert sands,
while Franz drives the car at wicked high speeds
over rugged terrain

(prone to mirage at every bend),
furrowed and riddled with little craters
which he skillfully dodges; undeterred, Franz keeps up
two snappy exchanges fore and aft, Alice in front bucketseat fast
with questions political and horticultural, Mort
to the rear, savoring tidbits of spiritual tutelage . . . Then, without
any least prior signal,
Mort starts gagging and puffing like a man caught
in the grip of seizure (heart attack,
stroke, convulsion?)—
at last, he's pointing and starts
waving his arms at some image in the desert.
Franz grinds to an abrupt halt, nearing the Bonaire rock monolith,
the historic volcano-upspewing itself.
Now bounding out the door, Mort finds himself weaving at a wide-
angled tilt, and holds
discourse with an apparition in the glare.
It's the wild donkey,

Oh, don't you see it?
It's telling me I must die, die, die—and only then may I return
as the man I was meant
to be. Oh, don't you hear the wild ass bray, he's scaring
the shit out of me . . . But Franz and Alice
are dumbfounded. They see nothing but blank desert, and glary flashes
of sun mirrored
back from standing pools, here & there. But no,
they don't see a donkey

yet they nod approval to Mort:

his *vision* is real enough, that they can see.

Now Mort is racing toward the huge black stone, circles it

partway, and starts to climb with keenest fervor. Soon he disappears,

and Alice—after a hiatus of ten minutes—

goes hunting for him. She hurries round and round the massive, haunted

black boulder, calling his name,

pleading with him to come back to us from wherever

he's descended, perhaps to the bowels

of the earth or such.

Franz pats her brow, consoles her—

not to worry. She relents, wandering about

the near desert area snapping pictures with her Nikon, but she mutters

aloud: *why did he so recklessly climb the rock,*

he must have fallen and knocked himself out, but where can he be? . . .

Then Mort emerges

from the rock's far side, serene and becalmed.

Well yes, he'd fallen,

but a controlled fall,

he is saying. He found the small ingress into the Bonaire Stone's

middle, and once within

that deep hollow where the temperature dropped to a cold

which made his teeth chatter and lips grow numb

with freeze, he felt a new outcropping emerge from his navel: the slimy

tube attached him

to the rock with a suction cup. Ecstasy surged

through him as he shook

from side to side, whereat he felt

the grand moment of *Shooting his Umbilicus!*

It took but a single moment, and he then felt lighter

than ever before in his life. A great weight had been lifted from him.

He rose, as if wings drew him upward, ever higher,

to the roof gap he'd entered some time before. When he climbed down,

his clothes had acquired the ash-
gray color of the rock . . . Franz extends his arm
around Mortimer's shoulder, and greets
his newborn entity,
            saying—*You've been reborn son
            of the rock, the body of the world, the planet—
the Mother Stone. You were first born from your mother's womb. Today,
            your second birth is mystical, as in the oldest
            legends. At last you become a true son of* terra firma. *Never again
shall you do harm
to the earth, or any of its blessed offspring.*
The next moment, Mort

                              fast bends down to kiss
this holy place. *Wherever you travel in the future,* Franz assures
                        him, *you'll always find
            holy ground beneath your feet to kiss, not only Bonaire's. . . .*
            Later that week, before winging home Mortimer
takes a stroll out to the peninsular shore rock where many young natives
                        have leapt, grimly
            falling to their deaths. A few champion athletes
                        had won high honors

for record dives from this lofty ridge,
            while others perished—cursed with broken necks,
            smashed spines, mako shark attacks . . . It's a gruesome
tally. And Mortimer, laying himself out flat on the ledge, commences
            to cry for the heroic dead, chanting prayerful
litany to the platform shelf to kill no more, to spare all future lives
of aspirant divers. He prays
and prays to the springboard rock to show mercy,
            mercy for the living . . . Next day, spooked
            by a gale-whipped flight
                        to Canada, he joins the Mystic
                        Order of the Rosicrucians, soon afterwards

becoming a High Master of that faith—whereupon he never once deigns
to practice the Law in courtrooms, having embraced
the planet's Innate Law. Wherever he goes, he'll bend to kiss the soil
at his feet. *If there's*
a patch of earth anyplace not holy, he sighs,
I do not know of it.